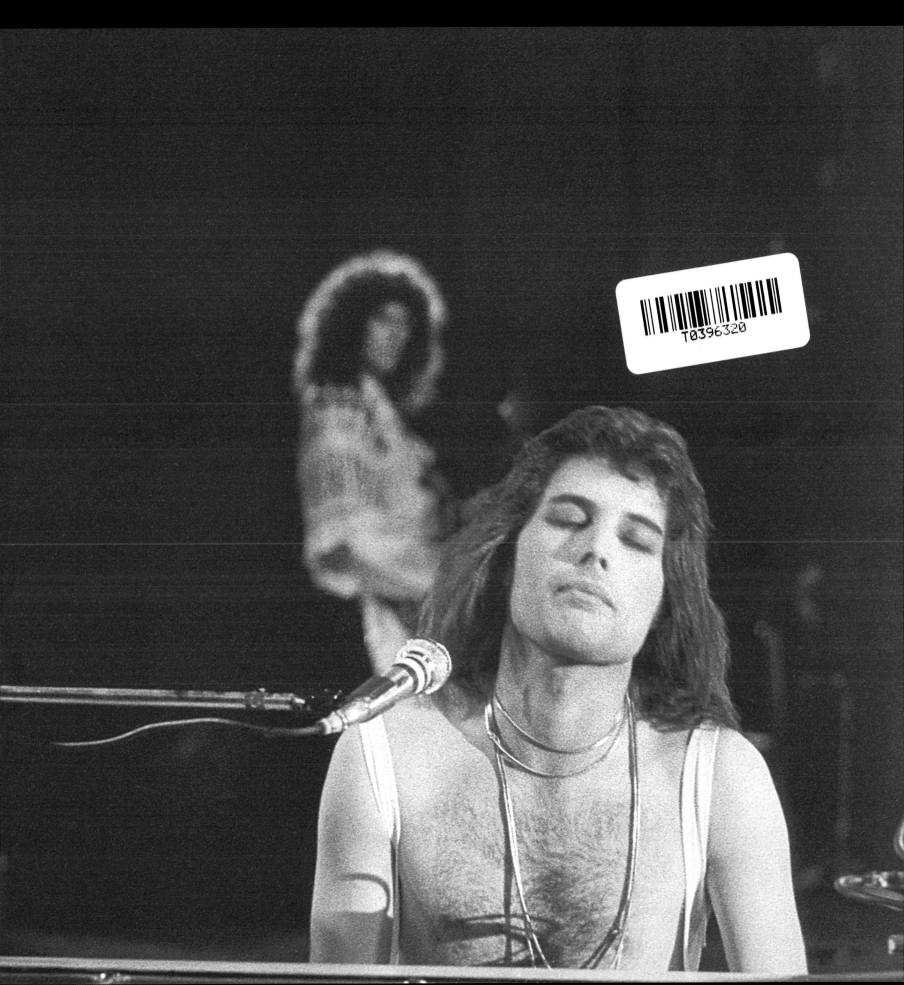

Queen
& A NIGHT AT THE OPERA 50 YEARS

Gillian G. Gaar

CONTENTS

Introduction | 6

1 The Context: Queen before 1975 | 8
2 The Sessions | 44
3 Side One | 64
4 Side Two | 78
5 The Release and Tour | 94
6 Sales and Awards | 120
7 Queen after *A Night at the Opera* | 130
8 Queen Is Dead, Long Live Queen! | 150

Tour Dates | 166
Bibliography | 167
Image Credits | 170
About the Author | 171
Index | 172

Introduction

"*AAAAAAYYYYY-OH!*"

The crowd responds in kind.

"*Aaaaaaaaayyyyyyyy-oh!*"

It's Freddie Mercury in the midst of the call-and-response routine that became a regular feature of Queen's concerts during their 1980s stadium years. It was a way to engage with the crowd and have a bit of fun, especially as Freddie's vocalizations become more and more elaborate, going up and down the scale at an increasing pace, finally bouncing straight up to a high note, which he holds for an extended period of time. The crowd always manages to replicate his vocal feats, to Freddie's obvious delight. He'll eventually bring the game to an end with an approving "All right!" or maybe a more jocular, "Fuck off!"

But the crowd that's singing back to Freddie tonight isn't a 1980s audience. It's November 9, 2023, the second show of a two-night stand in San Francisco, as the Queen + Adam Lambert "Rhapsody Tour" hits the West Coast. The audience is watching a film clip of Freddie from one of Queen's Wembley Stadium concerts in 1986, shown at the beginning of the encore. And their singing is just as raucous as that of the audience at the Wembley show over thirty-five years ago. Freddie Mercury might not be physically on the stage. But there's no doubt that his spirit fills the arena.

After an earlier stint by Paul Rodgers in the lead vocalist role, Adam Lambert joined Queen in 2011—twenty years after Freddie Mercury succumbed to AIDS at his London home at the age of forty-five. The remaining members of Queen thought it was the end of the band; bassist John Deacon essentially went into retirement. But guitarist Brian May and drummer Roger Taylor were open to the idea of creating a second act for the legendary band, one of the best-selling rock acts of all time.

It turned out that audiences were eager for them to return as well. And it's certainly no problem to put together a powerhouse show when you have an impressive catalog of hits to draw on like Queen does. "Radio Ga Ga." "Another One Bites the Dust." "Killer Queen." "Somebody to Love." "Under Pressure." "We Are the Champions." To mention a few.

The main set concludes with a song introduced by another film clip, from the video of Queen's most famous song: "Bohemian Rhapsody." A song that bucked convention by getting on the radio despite its being considered far too long for radio play. A song with a distinctive video at a time when artists who made promotional films for singles were the exception rather than the rule. And a song from the album that finally launched Queen into the heady realm of rock stardom: *A Night at the Opera*.

It was the album that changed everything for the band. Before its release, they were promising. Afterward, they had finally arrived. Hitting the top spot on the album and singles charts opened all the doors that had previously been closed to them. The future would hold more hit records, mammoth sales, record-setting tours. And even though they ceased touring in 1986, their final two albums still raced to the top of the charts in their native England (and a few other countries as well). Queen had become, and remain, an unbeatable act.

But the story of *A Night at the Opera* is about more than statistics, record sales, or the platinum awards received. It's a work of great musical versatility, encompassing vaudeville and hard rock, heartfelt balladry and mystical prog rock. It's a technical marvel as well, the band, and their equally adventurous coproducer, Roy Thomas Baker, pushing the studio technology of the day to its limits. It was the album where the band went for broke, putting their entire career on the line. As Brian May later observed, had it not succeeded, Queen would likely have ended. Instead, they hit the jackpot and have reaped the rewards ever since.

Landmark albums generate their own mythologies, and *A Night at the Opera* is no exception. But there's enough real drama in this tale that it doesn't require any further embellishments. It's the story of how a hardworking, iconoclastic foursome, operating at the peak of their creative powers, came together and drew on all their imagination, musical expertise, and ambition to make one of the most distinctive and acclaimed albums in rock history. An album that, fifty years on, is still regarded as a masterpiece.

Welcome to *A Night at the Opera*.

The cover for *A Night at the Opera* was the first time Queen's logo had been presented in full color.

1

The Context

QUEEN BEFORE 1975

"The whole group aimed for the top slot. We're not going to be content with anything else."

—FREDDIE MERCURY,
MELODY MAKER, DECEMBER 1974

(PREVIOUS) **By the time Queen recorded their fourth album, they were ready to, as Freddie put it, "aim for the top slot."**

(ABOVE) **Brian's (far right) first band, the Orwellian-named 1984, picked up gigs at local halls and pubs, even sharing a few bills with Jimi Hendrix.**

LONDON, NOVEMBER 1975. After months of hard work in six different studios, Queen had finally finished work on their fourth album. Or had they?

It was the evening *A Night at the Opera* was scheduled to be previewed for the press at Roundhouse Studios (since a *Melody Maker* reporter on hand at the preview noted that Queen had four days left to prepare for their UK tour, set to begin on November 14, the preview was probably held the night of November 9). A final mix had ostensibly been completed just hours before the 7 p.m. kickoff, the band's guitarist, Brian May, having stayed up all night to finish work on his epic track "The Prophet's Song." But the band remained unsatisfied; more work needed to be done. The preview would still be held, of course, in the best "show must go on" tradition. But afterward, Queen would head back into the studio to make some further changes to the album.

It was time that could've been spent rehearsing for their upcoming tour. But as Queen's lead singer Freddie Mercury had explained to many a journalist, "We're the fussiest band in the world, dear." And why shouldn't they be? This was the most important album of their career. In Brian May's words, it was make-or-break time—a moment they'd been building toward for five long years. If it took a little longer to get everything exactly right, so be it. This was a band that was not going to leave anything to chance.

QUEEN'S STORY BEGINS on a fall day in 1968, when Brian pinned up a card on a noticeboard at Imperial College, London, where he was studying physics and astronomy, looking for a "Mitch Mitchell/Ginger Baker type drummer." Brian and his friend Tim Staffell had been members of a group called 1984 that had recently broken up, and the two wanted to get a new group together.

Brian's friend Les Brown pointed out the ad to his flatmate, Roger Taylor, an aspiring drummer from Cornwall who was studying at Barts and The London School of Medicine and Dentistry, more as a means of getting to London than to seriously pursue a career as a dentist. Taylor's drums were still stored at his mother's home in Cornwall. But when he answered the ad, he got on well with May and Staffell, and his audition when his drums finally arrived was just a formality. "We thought he was the best drummer we'd ever seen," May later recalled. With Staffell as lead vocalist and bassist, and his friend Chris Smith on keyboards, the band Smile was born.

Roger promptly put his dental studies on hold. But the others still had academic ambitions. Brian had recently completed a bachelor of science in physics and mathematics at Imperial College (receiving his diploma on October 24, 1968, from the Queen Mother at the graduation ceremony held at London's Royal Albert Hall) and had stayed on to undertake postgraduate work. Staffell and Smith were studying at Ealing Technical College. Smith soon left the band, either of his own accord or because the other three preferred to work as a trio, depending on the account.

Smile played primarily in London but also ventured as far east as Truro, Cornwall, where Roger had connections. In 1969, the band's manager, Taylor's friend Peter Abbey, passed a demo tape to John Anthony, an A&R rep at Mercury Records. Anthony told Queen biographer Mark Blake he regarded the band as a "'Led Yes' because they had Yes's harmonies and Zeppelin's big riffs." But the band were offered a paltry deal to release only one single. The original songs "Earth" (written by Staffell) and "Step on Me" (cowritten by Staffell and May) were recorded at Trident Studios, Brian and Roger's first time in the studio where Queen would later launch their career. The single was released later in the year in the US only and promptly sank without a trace.

Though Smile soldiered on, they were making little progress beyond being a support act. On March 29, 1970, Staffell announced his departure, leaving Brian and Roger momentarily at loose ends. But there was already a replacement waiting patiently in the wings.

(LEFT) **Brian (standing at left) and other members of 1984 pose with a BMW Isetta. Where do the drums go?**

(ABOVE RIGHT) **Smile's only single; the first time Brian and Roger appeared on a record.**

THE CONTEXT

MAN OF CONTRADICTION:
Brian May

Brian May is seemingly a man of contradictions: the serious academic whose PhD dissertation is entitled *A Survey of Radial Velocities in the Zodiacal Dust Cloud,* and the rock 'n' roller who composed the rather less esoteric "Fat Bottomed Girls." In truth, he's just better at recognizing that they're all different facets of the human experience. Brian's skill was in integrating those aspects into one remarkable career.

Brian Harold May was born on July 19, 1947, in Hampton Hill, Middlesex, the only child of Harold and Ruth May, and grew up in Feltham, a suburb of London. His father, who'd been an amateur musician, passed on his interest in music to his son, who started out on ukulele, suffered through a few piano lessons, and was finally given his first guitar, a Spanish acoustic, at age seven.

Brian was also an intelligent child, developing a keen interest in astronomy. But while he never neglected his studies, music increasingly became his dominant interest. Skiffle musician Lonnie Donegan's "Rock Island Line" inspired him to play music, and he was equally captivated by Buddy Holly and the Crickets. He was drawn to guitarists (Les Paul, Django Reinhardt) and followed UK acts like Tommy Steele and the Shadows. When he couldn't afford an electric guitar to emulate his idols, he and his father set about making one, the famous "Red Special."

He formed his first band, 1984 (named after George Orwell's classic dystopian novel), with friends from school, playing at local halls and small clubs, staying with the group after he left for London's Imperial College in the fall of 1965. As the decade progressed, there were new guitarists to admire: Jeff Beck, Eric Clapton, and especially Jimi Hendrix, whom, Brian declared, "came along and destroyed everyone." Eventually 1984 would share the bill with Hendrix twice, but Brian had no personal interactions with the legendary musician.

In 1967, Brian got his first studio experience when one of 1984's members arranged to record demos at Thames Television's studios in Teddington. That same year, he also recorded demos with his friend Bill Richards' band The Left Handed Marriage, working in the famed Abbey Road Studios on one occasion. He quit 1984 the following year but soon returned to performing with 1984's lead singer, Tim Staffell, the two forming the band Smile.

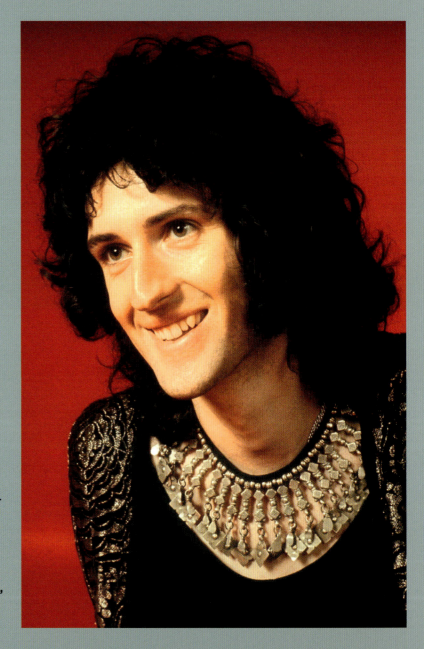

Brian May, the PhD astrophysicist who penned "Fat Bottomed Girls." Man of contradictions or simply well rounded?

Like many a British lad of the 1950s, Brian was inspired to pick up the guitar upon hearing the skiffle King Lonnie Donegan.

"Brian is one of the most eccentric people I have ever met."

—ROGER TAYLOR ON BRIAN MAY

(ABOVE) **Like Freddie, Brian took time from Queen to explore occasional side projects, recording with such friends as Eddie Van Halen.**

(OPPOSITE) **In 2002, Brian opened the concert commemorating Queen Elizabeth II's Golden Jubilee by playing "God Save the Queen" on the roof of Buckingham Palace.**

Smile, of course, evolved into Queen. While Brian wrote stirring rock anthems like "We Will Rock You" and "Tie Your Mother Down" for the band, songs like "Leaving Home Ain't Easy" and "Sleeping on the Sidewalk" suggested he felt conflicted about the rock star life. In an astonishing admission to *Mojo*'s David Thomas, he described being in Queen as "wonderful, magical," but added the experience "came close to destroying us all. I'm not being dramatic. I think it truly fucked us up in the way that only a sort of out-of-world experience like that can do."

With most of his energies focused on Queen, there were few side projects. In 1983, he released the single "Star Fleet" (a TV cartoon theme song), recorded with such friends as Eddie Van Halen. He also appeared on albums by Black Sabbath, Billy Squier, and Roger's band The Cross, as well as producing a parody version of "Bohemian Rhapsody" by the comic rock act Bad News. He also produced actress Anita Dobson's 1988 album *Talking of Love*, a liaison that led to the end of his first marriage (he and Dobson married in 2000).

When Freddie died in 1991, the same year as Brian's father, he later said, "I felt like life was over . . . I felt like I was losing everything." He coped by launching a solo career, releasing three albums, and touring as a solo act. And the revival of Queen in the new century happily took him back to the kind of large-scale touring he'd thought had come to an end with Mercury's death.

Outside of Queen, he regularly makes guest appearances in concert and on record with numerous acts: Lady Gaga, Meat Loaf, Genesis, and Kerry Ellis, producing her debut album and touring with her. His lifelong interest in stereoscopic photography led to his establishing the London Stereoscopic Company, which publishes books on the subject. And he finished his PhD dissertation (on interplanetary dust in the solar system), becoming "Dr. May" in 2007.

One of the proudest (and most nerve-wracking) performances of his life came in 2002, when he opened the "Party at the Palace" concert commemorating Queen Elizabeth II's Golden Jubilee by playing "God Save the Queen" on the roof of Buckingham Palace. In 2005, he was appointed a Commander of the Order of the British Empire (CBE) and was given a knighthood in 2023, both honors granted for his music and charity work.

Despite all his varied interests, Brian knows where his strengths lie: "I'm a much better musician than astronomer. I think the world got the right choice." Millions of fans around the globe would agree with him about that.

THE CONTEXT

FREDDIE BULSARA had become acquainted with Brian, and then Roger, through his friendship with Tim Staffell. He was a regular at both 1984 and Smile shows, sometimes gaining free entrance by helping the bands with their gear. He also didn't hesitate to offer advice, suggesting the band dress with a bit more style or make changes to a particular song's arrangement. In Brian's recollection, Freddie already dressed like a rock star, "but the kind of rock star you hadn't seen before—really flamboyant and androgynous."

It was obvious that Freddie very much wanted to be in a band himself, but there was no way to do that in Smile. So for the time being, he involved himself in other projects. After graduating from Ealing Technical College with a degree in graphic design, he picked up occasional work as a designer. He also ran a stall at Kensington Market along with Roger, initially selling his own art and even copies of his thesis on Jimi Hendrix (like Brian and Roger, Freddie was a keen Hendrix fan). The two later moved on to selling used clothing.

He eventually did brief stints in two bands. In 1969, he was taken on as lead singer for Ibex, a band from St. Helens, outside Liverpool, who'd come to London hoping to make it in the music industry. At Freddie's instigation, the band later changed their name to Wreckage but had broken up by the end of the year. Two key things happened

(ABOVE) **At the age of eight, Freddie was sent to St. Peter's School in Panchgani, India. Until age sixteen, he would only see his parents for a month during the summer.**

(RIGHT) **Freddie, in front, second from left, with the members of Ibex and friends on August 23, 1969.**

(OPPOSITE) **Freddie learned to play guitar, feeling it would help him with his songwriting.**

(RIGHT) **Freddie's work in college bands such as Sour Milk Sea served as apprenticeships for the more serious work ahead.**

(OPPOSITE) **Biba was one of London's most fashionable boutiques. The young, hip staff, like shop assistant Valerie Allen, seen here, was as much of a draw as the clothing.**

during this period. First, while the band were still called Ibex, Brian and Roger joined them during the encore at a show in Liverpool on September 9—the first time the three future members of Queen played together. Also, at a show in Widnes on November 24, the base of Freddie's mic stand came off. He carried on singing without it, creating what would become a signature prop: a shortened mic stand that he could wield to great dramatic effect. As he later told a friend, "You must have a gimmick."

In 1970, Freddie answered an ad in the British music weekly *Melody Maker* and joined a band called Sour Milk Sea. But the group fell apart pretty quickly. Not that Freddie was too upset; the timing was finally right for him to join up with Brian and Roger in Smile.

"We didn't see a great singer or musician first of all," Brian later admitted. "He was very wild and unsophisticated. We just saw someone who had incredible belief and charisma, and we liked him."

Mike Grose, a friend of Roger's who'd filled in on a few Smile dates after Staffell's departure, was tapped to play bass, and the new configuration made its debut on June 27, 1970, in Truro. The gig had already been booked under Smile's name, but that was soon to change; by their next confirmed show, July 18 at Imperial College, they'd become Queen.

It was Freddie's suggestion. No one else liked it. But the other names they'd come up with—Rich Kids, The Grand Dance, Build Your Own Boat—hadn't been any better. The main concern was that it was just too camp to be taken seriously. But Freddie was

(ABOVE) **Queen often played Truro, in Cornwall, where Roger was from. The poster is for a show on August 21, 1971, at Truro's Tregye Country Club.**

(OPPOSITE) **The band sits for promotional photos in 1973. In November 1972, they had signed management, recording, and publishing contracts with, respectively, Trident Audio Productions, Neptune Productions, and Trident / Feldman Music.**

insistent, playing down the innuendo by emphasizing how "regal" the name was. "It's a strong name, very universal and immediate," he later told *Melody Maker*. "It had a lot of visual potential and was open to all sorts of interpretations. I was certainly aware of the gay connotations, but that was just one facet of it."

No one thought then that those "gay connotations" necessarily applied to Freddie. He dated women at the time and would enter into a long-term relationship with Mary Austin, who worked at the fashionable clothing boutique Biba and had previously briefly dated Brian. And with the rise of glam rock in the 1970s, androgyny and gender-bending had become very *au courant*. As Freddie himself admitted in an interview, "I play on the bisexual thing."

It took a while for Queen to stabilize their lineup. Mike Grose soon left, replaced by Barry Mitchell, referred by a mutual acquaintance of Taylor's. But Mitchell left in early 1971; like Grose, he didn't see much future in Queen. The band took out an ad in *Melody Maker* and ended up hiring Douglas Bogie, who lasted two shows before he was ousted for his overenthusiastic performance style (Brian: "He jumped up and down in a manner most incongruous").

Finally, a mutual friend introduced them to John Deacon, who was studying electronics at Chelsea College and had previously played in bands in his hometown of Oadby, a suburb of Leicester. He would prove to be the archetypal "quiet bassist," a man of few words but one who fit in instantly. He made his live debut with Queen on July 2, 1971, at Ewell Technical College in Surrey. "It's nice to have that cross-section between the four of us, so when we come together, it's quite a good blend," Freddie observed to journalist Robert Duncan of the band's disparate personalities. "It would be awfully boring if we were all the same. . . . We are totally individual, but our ideas just seem to blend somewhere along the line, which is important."

A few months after Deacon joined, Queen got the chance to make a professional demo. Brian had contacted Terry Yeadon, a studio engineer who'd previously worked on demos for Smile. Yeadon was now working for De Lane Lea Music Centre in Wembley and was looking for a band to test the facility's equipment in exchange for a free demo. Queen happily signed on and ended up recording five original songs (versions of which would appear on their debut album). Ken Testi, who'd managed Ibex, took the demo around to London's record companies but received only a single offer (Charisma offered the band £25,000). Despite their impoverished circumstances, Queen turned it down, confident they could land a more substantial deal.

But interest was about to come from another quarter. John Anthony, who'd signed Smile to Mercury, was now working at Trident Studios and had formed a new company, Neptune Productions, with engineers/producers Roy Thomas Baker and Robin Cable, who also worked at Trident. Anthony had suggested his two partners check out De Lane Lea's studios, and they stopped by when Queen was recording. Baker was immediately taken by their material; the spirited "Keep Yourself Alive," in particular, sounded like a potential hit. "I just thought that here was a band doing something new and fresh," he told *Sound on Sound*.

On hearing the final demo, Anthony was in agreement, and they tipped off Trident's owners, Norman and Barry Sheffield. The Sheffields had opened Trident Studios in 1968 in the midst of London's lively Soho neighborhood and quickly attracted such clients as the Beatles, David Bowie, and Lou Reed. Barry went to see Queen live and was not only impressed with their original material but also the band's campy rendition of "Big Spender" (from the musical *Sweet Charity*).

A late-December 1973 handbill advertises a gig with fellow British rockers 10cc.

The Sheffields wanted to work with Queen, but it took a while to sort out the details, so the band put live performances on hold, playing just five gigs in 1972. Brian and John were still at college (Brian taking on a teaching job for extra money), Roger enrolled at the Polytechnic of North London to study biology and live off a student grant, and Freddie worked for another vendor at Kensington Market and took on the occasional graphic design job. They had no interest in burning out playing small clubs. As Roger told *Melody Maker*, "We all wanted to play big, big concerts, and didn't want to get stuck in that circuit for years and years, which is so easy to do, no matter how good you are."

There was now also an album to make. Though the contracts with Trident were still being negotiated, Queen began recording their debut at the studio, sharing production duties with John Anthony and Roy Thomas Baker (Anthony dropped out when he became ill). Sessions continued through October. Since no deal was yet in place, the band were confined to working during the studio's down time—generally the middle of the night.

Though not yet fully developed, elements of Queen's distinctive sound are evident on the final album, most notably their trademark three-part harmonies, with Brian, Freddie, and Roger taking the low, middle, and high parts, respectively. "As soon as the three of us sang a line, it already sounded quite big," May later observed. "You double-track that and it sounds very big." Freddie's penchant for theatrical fantasy is clear in song titles like "My Fairy King" and "Great King Rat;" Brian's more contemplative side is heard on moody numbers like "The Night Comes Down," contrasting with his flashy guitar solo on "Doing All Right" (a Smile song cowritten with Tim Staffell); Roger takes a headlong dive into "Modern Times Rock 'n' Roll." Queen's influences (hard rock, glam, prog rock) are clear, but the band put their own spin on them, one reason reviewers would find it hard to describe what sort of a group they were.

On November 1, 1972, Queen signed management, recording, and publishing contracts with, respectively, Trident Audio Productions, Neptune Productions, and Trident/Feldman Music. According to Norman Sheffield, he was reluctant to enter into a management agreement with the band, fearing a conflict of interest, but Mercury, in particular, was insistent. It was similar to the arrangement Bruce Springsteen made with his first manager, Mike Appel, who looked after his client's management, recording, and publishing interests—which ended up in a lawsuit when the conflicts of interest became all too apparent. Queen had taken their first step down a similar path.

The band members were also put on a retainer of £25 a week. Queen was steadily becoming their full-time occupation. Roger had completed his degree in biology. John got his degree in electronics but, hedging his bets, stayed on for postgraduate work. Brian quit his teaching job and finally put work on his PhD thesis aside, thinking, "If I don't quit this and give the group a chance I'll end up regretting it." Or, as John Anthony put it to him, "Look, Brian, you can study the stars or you can be one!"

ENIGMATIC FRONTMAN: Freddie Mercury

Despite being Queen's most flamboyant member, Freddie Mercury remained an enigma even to those who knew him. "No one really knew Freddie," Roger Taylor observed. "He was shy, gentle, and kind. He wasn't the person he put over on stage." Whether on or off stage, Queen's main man always kept himself at a distance. As Roger admitted elsewhere, "He was a mystery."

Perhaps it was not surprising, for Freddie was always something of an outsider. He was born Farrokh Bulsara in Zanzibar, an island off the coast of Africa (now part of Tanzania), on September 5, 1946, to Bomi and Jer Bulsara; he also had a younger sister, Kashmira. His parents were Parsi Indians, of Persian descent and adherents of the Zoroastrian faith. His father worked as a High Court cashier for the British government (Zanzibar was a British protectorate at the time), and the family enjoyed a comfortable living, able to employ servants.

At the age of eight, he was sent to St. Peter's School in Panchgani, India; until the age of sixteen, Freddie would only see his parents for a month during the summer. As he grew up, he became increasingly self-conscious about his protruding front teeth, due to his having four extra back teeth, which led to his classmates calling him "Bucky." He also felt lonely, though he later said that being at boarding school taught him how to "fend for myself."

But he was not without friends. In the first step in inventing a new public persona, he was also given a friendlier nickname by teachers and students: Freddie. His interest in music was noted, and he began taking piano lessons. He became keenly interested in rock 'n' roll when it arrived in the mid-1950s, and Queen's sets usually featured an Elvis Presley or Little Richard cover. He also formed his first band, the Hectics, while at school with his fellow students, playing piano and singing backing vocals.

To his parents' disappointment, Freddie left school in 1963 after failing his exams. But the family soon had greater worries. Due to the civil unrest that followed in wake of Zanzibar gaining its independence, the Bulsaras left for England in 1964, settling in Feltham, a suburb of London (very close to Brian May's home, though the families never met). It was the beginning of a new era for Freddie, who rarely spoke about his childhood from this point on. Determined to pursue a career in the arts, he briefly attended Isleworth Polytechnic to get sufficient credits to transfer to the Ealing Technical College in September 1966.

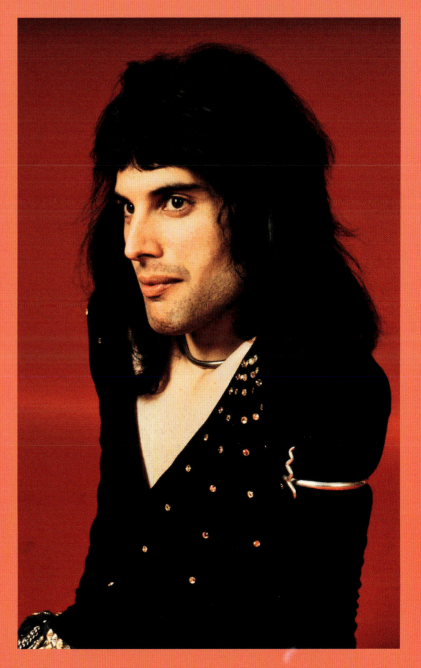

Flamboyant though he may have been onstage, Freddie always kept himself at distance when offstage.

THE CONTEXT

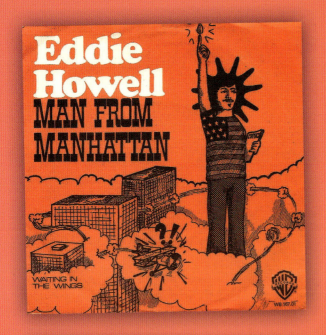

The most fortuitous part about his years at Ealing was that he met Tim Staffell, which eventually led to his joining Queen, his tenure in the bands Ibex (later Wreckage) and Sour Milk Sea serving as apprenticeships for the more serious work that lay ahead. Along with his musical skills (his love of classical music was a key element of Queen's songs), Freddie understood the importance of having a strong visual image, telling producer John Anthony he wanted the band to be the audio equivalent of the high-society magazine *Queen*. He worked closely with the designers who created the costumes for the band, Freddie's outfits naturally being the most elaborate. His belief in Queen was unassailable—he was the one who always insisted the band would not just be successful, but stars.

Once he'd achieved that success, Freddie took on a few side projects. He dabbled in production, producing and performing on Eddie Howell's 1976 single "The Man from Manhattan" (also featuring Brian May on guitar). He danced at a special performance by London's Royal Ballet company in 1979. He cowrote (with Giorgio Moroder) "Love Kills" for the 1984 rock soundtrack created for the silent film *Metropolis*, released as a Freddie Mercury "solo" single though the other members of Queen all appear on it. The same year saw a failed songwriting collaboration with Michael Jackson.

On his own, he had success in the UK and Europe with the singles "I Was Born to Love You" and "The Great Pretender," and the albums *Mr. Bad Guy* and *Barcelona*. The latter album, a collaboration with one of his favorite opera singers, Montserrat Caballé, was a project close to his heart.

He never spoke about any conflict he may have felt about keeping his private life under wraps; at the time of his death, more people were aware of his former girlfriend Mary Austin than his current boyfriend Jim Hutton. But it was typical of the control he maintained over every other area of his life. And for all his comments about his music being nothing more than "disposable pop," he was also a man who cared very much about his legacy. "When I'm dead, I want to be remembered as a musician of some worth and substance," he told *Circus* in 1977. That's a hope that has certainly come true.

After achieving success with Queen, Freddie pursued side projects and guest appearances apart from the band, including performing on Eddie Howell's 1976 single, "The Man from Manhattan."

"He was a rock star, always. He was a born rock star."

—BRIAN MAY ON FREDDIE MERCURY

(ABOVE) **Freddie's interest in art led to his being the band member who was the most concerned with Queen's visual image.**

(RIGHT) **The album *Barcelona* was a project close to Freddie's heart—a collaboration with one of his favorite opera singers, Montserrat Caballé.**

BRITAIN AT LARGE got its first taste of Queen on February 15, 1973, when the band's four-song appearance on *Sounds of the Seventies* was broadcast on BBC Radio 1. Soon after, Trident landed deals with EMI Records in the UK and Elektra in the US. But the first record released with Freddie's voice on it wouldn't be by Queen but a single credited to the fictitious "Larry Lurex" (a play on the name of glam singer Gary Glitter). Trident's engineer Robin Cable, wanting to flex his muscles as a producer, had been working on a single emulating Phil Spector's famed Wall of Sound production style: "I Can Hear Music," a song previously recorded by the Ronettes and the Beach Boys. Cable roped in Mercury to provide vocals, as well as May and Taylor on guitar and drums. The single was released in June 1973, with a cover of Dusty Springfield's "Goin' Back" on the B-side, and promptly disappeared.

Queen's first proper single, "Keep Yourself Alive" (featuring May's first-ever multi-tracked guitar solo), followed on July 6 in the UK and October 8 in the US, and it failed to do any better despite some good reviews. *Queen* was released July 13 in the UK, September 4 in the US. The cover featured the debut of Queen's logo, designed by Freddie. The front cover had a simple rendition of the logo; just the band's name with a crown resting inside the Q. The back cover had a more elaborate variation: the Q with its crown surrounded by characters representing the zodiac signs of each member (lions for May and Taylor, both Leos, a crab for Deacon, a Cancer, and maidens for Freddie, a Virgo), with a phoenix rising from the flames at the top.

The back cover also debuted Freddie's new name; having signed with Trident as "Freddie Bulsara," the cover credited him as Freddie Mercury. John Deacon was credited as "Deacon John," having been momentarily persuaded that it "sounded better" (he reverted to John Deacon on every subsequent Queen album). Roger was credited with his full name, "Roger Meddows-Taylor," making him sound like a member of the landed gentry. Those who read the credits all the way through would've also come across this line: ". . . and nobody played synthesizer," added because of people thinking the more ornate sounds were coming from a keyboard and not May's guitar. A similar notation would appear on every album through *News of the World*.

In the US, *Queen* reached #83, which was a decent showing, considering the band were completely unknown in the States. *Rolling Stone* even called the album "superb." But reaching #32 in the UK was a disappointment. So was the fact that no radio stations could be persuaded to add "Keep Yourself Alive" to their playlists. The band was further put off by the tone of their media coverage in the UK music press. Due to their lack of live concerts, they were written off in some quarters for being all hype and no substance. There were even speculations they used session musicians in the studio. Nick Kent, in a crushing review in the music weekly *New Musical Express* (*NME*), wrote that the band suffered from a "devastating paucity of originality or vision" and described their album's songs as "really embarrassing."

And then there was their name, which Kent had written off as "stupid." For all Freddie's protestations that the "gay connotations" were just "one facet" of it, that was the aspect the media loved to focus on, resulting in headlines like "No limp wrists on this Queen!" It was an element that readily lent itself to innuendo, amplified over the years by Freddie's penchant for camp affectations like dropping "dear" and "darling" into his sentences, musing that he'd like to be carried onstage by "six nubile slaves," and answering questions about his sexuality with a cheery, "I'm gay as a daffodil, dear!" (and then posing holding the flower in front of Buckingham Palace). Even the supportive pieces carried a whiff of condescension, as in Michael Benton's story for *Melody Maker*: "But

(OPPOSITE TOP LEFT) **Freddie's vinyl debut came not on a Queen record, but on a one-off side project single credited to "Larry Lurex" (spoofing the name of glam singer Gary Glitter). The single also featured Brian and Roger.**

(OPPOSITE BOTTOM) **Two editions of Queen's self-titled debut album. The cover was designed by Freddie, and featured him holding his microphone stand aloft.**

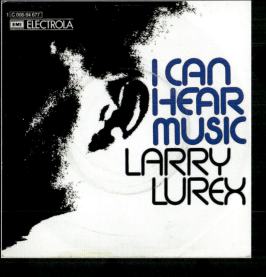
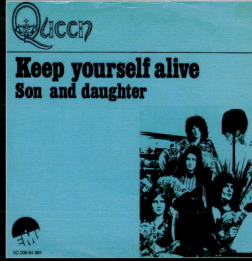

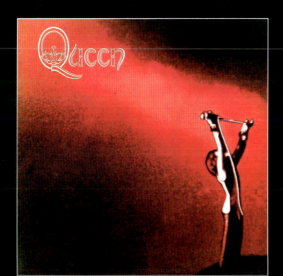
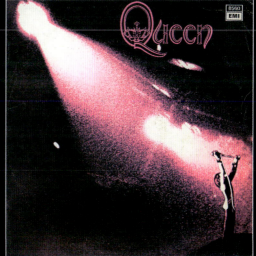

(LEFT) Queen rehearsing for their fall 1973 tour, which included their first dates outside the UK.

(ABOVE) Photographer Mick Rock first met Queen while they were recording *Queen II*, and conceived this striking image for the album's cover. Note that the vinyl edition of the album does not have the "Side White" designation used on the record labels in other countries.

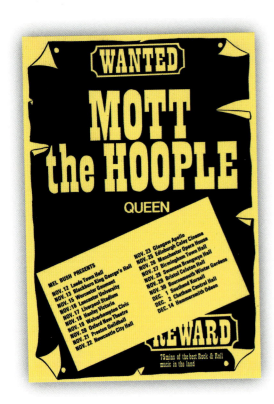

a word of warning—don't try it on with these Queens. They're tough, and their music is very masculine. . . . Not outstandingly gay, I think you'll agree." As Queen's popularity grew, there would always be some critics who never hesitated to use any avenue to attack the band, and Freddie's ambiguous sexuality was a prime target. Queen was not destined to have comfortable relations with the Fourth Estate.

Within a month of their debut album's release, the band were back at Trident working on the follow up, *Queen II*, again coproducing with Roy Thomas Baker (Robin Cable coproduced on some tracks). This was the album where the band's sound began coming more into focus. "I think that set our direction more than anything else," Brian told *Melody Maker*. "*Queen II* was a point where all the adventurous ideas came out." The band were excited about the prospect of stretching the boundaries of what could be done in a recording studio. "If there are any ideas that you've had that you can't use with boring, human-type bands," Freddie told Baker, "we'll try them out on this."

The result was a wildly imaginative album, lavishly packaged in a gatefold sleeve, with a black outer sleeve and a dazzling white for the inner gatefold. The color scheme extended to the album itself, whose sides were labeled "Side White" and "Side Black." Side White primarily featured May's songs, opening with the stately "Procession," an instrumental that sounded more like classical music. "Brian was already onto something different, in terms of trying to orchestrate his guitars in a different way to how most people would approach it," Baker told *Sound on Sound*. "We never thought of Brian's guitar as a raunchy instrument, like most guitarists do; it was an orchestral instrument."

Side Black was all Freddie, and a phantasmagorical delight. The fearsome "Ogre Battle" featured all manner of audio effects, such as backward cymbals and drums, as well as the first appearance of the mighty gong that would later appear in "Bohemian Rhapsody." "The Fairy Feller's Master Stroke" celebrated the Richard Dadd painting of the same name, which depicted kings and queens, gnomes and satyrs, and, as per the lyric, a variety of "quaere fellows" (Freddie even took the band, and Baker, to see the painting at the Tate Gallery). May's "White Queen (As It Began)" was matched by Mercury's extravagant number about her doppelganger: "The March of the Black Queen." "*Queen II* was like the 'kitchen sink' of every known Queen effect," Baker later observed.

The band were also breaking new ground as a live act. The fall brought their first foreign dates, with gigs in Bonn-Bad Godesberg, Germany, on October 13 and Luxembourg City, Luxembourg, the following night. On November 12, they began their first UK tour, opening for Mott the Hoople, something they regarded as a valuable learning experience. "Mott taught us how to behave as a band and how to survive over a long period," Mercury told *NME*. The tour closed on December 14 with two shows at London's Rainbow Theatre, the second show added after the first sold out.

But things got off to a rougher start in 1974. The band had received injections in advance of their first tour to Australia, and Brian's arm developed gangrene due to the use of a dirty needle. He was still feeling unwell when the band arrived in Melbourne to play the Sunbury Pop Festival on January 27 (some accounts say February 2, but the festival ran from January 25 to 28 in 1974). Freddie was also under the weather due to an ear infection, and there were conflicts with the local crew, who weren't allowed to operate Queen's equipment. The band acquitted themselves well but were denied an encore when the emcee goaded the crowd by saying, "Do you want more of those Pommy bastards? Or do you want a good old Aussie band?" The band canceled their scheduled performance for the next day and quickly headed for home. Freddie vowed that when they returned, they'd be the biggest band in the world, a far-fetched claim at the time.

(LEFT AND OPPOSITE) **"Mott taught us how to behave as a band,"** Freddie said of Queen's experience opening for Mott the Hoople in 1973 and 1974, with both bands always ready for some backstage shenanigans. Queen later namechecked Mott in their song "Now I'm Here."

(BOTTOM) **The band pauses for a photo at London's Heathrow Airport on January 31, 1974, upon their return from a rocky first trip to Australia.**

THE CONTEXT

THE RELUCTANT ROCK STAR: John Deacon

John Deacon once observed that when he first joined Queen, he kept his own counsel because he was "the new boy." In a band with such larger-than-life characters, it seemed safer to keep his head down until he'd settled in. But even after he'd been in the group for years, he remained Queen's most reticent member and the very definition of the archetypal bass player: strong but silent. And capable of writing some of Queen's most memorable numbers.

John Richard Deacon was born on August 19, 1951, in Leicester, where he lived until he was nine. He, his younger sister, Julie, and his parents, Arthur and Lilian, then moved to nearby Oadby, and his father died the following year. His musical career began when he was given a toy "Official Tommy Steele Gitar" [sic] at age seven. In 1963, inspired by the Beatles' records, he bought his first proper instrument, an acoustic guitar, and taught himself to play. In addition to music, he also had a keen interest in electronics, which would serve him well in Queen's early days.

In 1965, John joined his first band, The Opposition (later The New Opposition), first playing rhythm guitar, then moving to bass. The band played cover songs of popular hits at local dances, though John sometimes had to miss a gig because his mother wouldn't allow him to play in pubs. In 1969, the band, now called Art, put up the money to record a single, which featured an original number, "Transit 3." No copies have made their way to the public.

When John left for London's Chelsea College that fall to pursue a career in electronics, he left his bass behind. But he missed playing music and brought the instrument with him when he returned to college after the summer break. Once he'd joined Queen, he still kept up with his studies, not fully certain of the band's future success: "I knew there was something but I wasn't convinced of it until possibly the *Sheer Heart Attack* album."

The band quickly came to appreciate John's steadfast temperament. Before they could afford full-time roadies, John's knowledge of electronics helped them look after their gear. He kept an eye on the band's business matters too. "The rest of the group won't do anything unless John says it's alright," Freddie explained to a reporter. And he wasn't afraid to hold his ground. When he found he'd been credited as "Deacon John" on the cover of their first album, he made sure his names were in the correct order on *Queen II*—and every Queen album after.

(RIGHT TOP AND BOTTOM) John with his first band, the Opposition, later the New Opposition (at the top in the first photo, at the far right in the second). He started out playing guitar in the band before moving permanently to bass.

John made his songwriting debut on Queen's third album, when the short but sweet "Misfire" appeared on *Sheer Heart Attack*, the very album that made him think the band might have a future. He was never very prolific, but after "You're My Best Friend," he's best known for crafting the immediately recognizable bass line for "Under Pressure," steering Queen into the realm of funk with "Another One Bites the Dust," and writing the song ("I Want to Break Free") that resulted in what was arguably Queen's most memorable video after "Bohemian Rhapsody."

Unlike Queen's other members, he wasn't interested in launching a solo career. His only solo release was the single "No Turning Back," which he cowrote for the 1986 film *Biggles* (based on W. E. Johns's series of books about a dashing pilot) and released under the name the Immortals (both the single and film failed to achieve liftoff). He also cowrote and appeared on Man Friday & Jive Junior's 1983 single "Picking Up Sounds," as well as on records by Elton John, Ian and Belinda, SAS Band, and the solo releases of his Queen bandmates.

But in general, when he wasn't working with Queen, John preferred the company of his family. He was the first member of the band to get married and the only member whose marriage has lasted (he and wife Veronica went on to have six children). Despite his involvement with the band's initial post-Freddie endeavors, for John, Queen came to an end with Freddie's death, and in 1997, following the recording session for Queen's "No-One But You (Only the Good Die Young)," he withdrew from public life completely. He was a no-show when Queen was inducted into the Rock and Roll Hall of Fame in 2001 and has declined offers to rejoin his bandmates in both the Queen + Paul Rodgers and Queen + Adam Lambert lineups.

Nor does he see the other members of Queen. In 2014, Roger told *Rolling Stone* John was "a little fragile and he just didn't want to know anything about talking to the people in the music business or whatever. That's fair enough. We respect that."

"He still keeps an eye on the finances, though," Brian added. "We don't undertake anything financial without talking to him."

Freddie would surely approve.

(ABOVE RIGHT) Queen's bassist during the band's four-night stand at New York city's Beacon Theatre in February 1976.

(RIGHT) John's distinctive bassline in "Under Pressure" has been sampled by numerous artists over the years.

"Ah, yes, the sonic volcano."

—BRIAN MAY ON JOHN DEACON

There was a turn for the better the following month. When David Bowie canceled an appearance on the UK television music program *Top of the Pops*, the show's producer, Robin Nash, put in an emergency call to EMI's head of promotion, Ronnie Fowler. Queen was one of Fowler's favorite up-and-coming bands, and he wasted no time in plugging their upcoming single, the robust "Seven Seas of Rhye." The band were reluctant to appear—*Top of the Pops* wasn't a showcase for serious musicians—but the exposure would be invaluable, and they eventually agreed to make a prerecorded appearance, miming, as per union rules, to a newly recorded backing track (though it was claimed the band used their original backing track without anyone noticing).

The performance aired on February 21; the band watched the show on a television in the window of an electronics shop in London's Kensington neighborhood, no one yet owning a TV. The single was rush-released soon after; Freddie, ever meticulous, noticed the wrong mix had been used on promo copies and insisted they be withdrawn and replaced with the correct mix. It became their first hit, peaking at #10 in the UK (though failing to chart in the US). The band's growing success led Freddie to quit working at Kensington Market; John would soon give up his postgraduate studies.

Having a hit single provided a nice boost to Queen's first headlining UK tour, which began March 1 in Blackpool. The release of *Queen II* followed on March 8, with US release on April 9. Reviews were mixed. "The band with the worst name have capped that dubious achievement by bringing out the worst album for some time," griped the UK music weekly *Record Mirror*. *Rolling Stone* was equally unimpressed, calling "Side Black" a "lyrically muddled fairy-tale world with none of Genesis's wit or sophistication . . . the album remains a floundering and sadly unoriginal affair." It still became the band's first hit album in the UK, peaking at #5 and cracking the US Top 50 at #49. As Julie Webb presciently noted in *NME*, "Queen are big business and though you may hate them, they're gonna confound you by being huge."

The tour wrapped up on April 2 in Birmingham. Two weeks later, the band flew to the US for their first stateside tour, again opening for Mott the Hoople. Unfortunately, Brian's health problems continued, and he developed hepatitis, leading to the band pulling out of the tour after a May 11 show at New York's Uris Theater. Then, while working on their next album, Brian was again hospitalized, suffering from a duodenal ulcer. His continued absences left him worried he might be kicked out of the band. But Freddie consoled him when visiting him in the hospital: "Don't worry, darling. We can't do it without you."

Queen began work on their third album, *Sheer Heart Attack*, in July 1974, with sessions running through September. It marked the first time they worked outside of Trident, with Roy Thomas Baker again on board. "I regard *Sheer Heart Attack* as the most polished Queen album, the most finished product, in the sense that we were playing better," Brian told *Melody Maker* in 1976, an assessment the rest of the band readily agreed with. "The writing was better, the recording had more aggression, and the whole thing was beginning to attain a sort of grandeur," Roger later told *Uncut*. Freddie was more puckish when talking with *NME*'s Julie Webb at the time of the album's release: "We're still the dandies we started out to be. We're just showing people we're not merely a load of poofs, that we are capable of other things."

(ABOVE) **After playing a string of dates opening for Mott the Hoople at New York's Uris Theater in May 1974, Queen prematurely left the tour, due to Brian's ill health.**

(RIGHT) **Mick Rock, who'd photographed the cover of *Queen II*, also took the cover shot of *Sheer Heart Attack*. The album featured Queen's first big hit, "Killer Queen."**

THE CONTEXT 35

 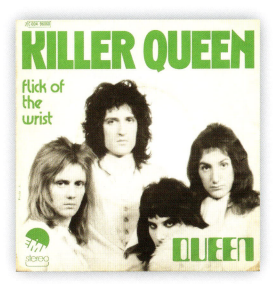

(LEFT) **Queen *en route* to the Continent on November 22, 1974, for a short European tour.**

(OPPOSITE) **Queen performing (or rather, miming) their hit single "Killer Queen" on Britain's popular music show *Top of the Pops*.**

It also delivered the band's first solid hit single, with Mercury's "Killer Queen," released October 11 in the UK, October 21 in the US. It was a bright pop confection, cheerfully namedropping Moët et Chandon, Marie Antoinette, Nikita Khrushchev, and John F. Kennedy, all in the first verse. "It's about a high-class call girl. I'm trying to say that classy people can be whores as well," Freddie told Julie Webb, making it something of an updated version of his encore number "Big Spender" (Simon Reynolds, in his book *Shock and Awe*, observed that Mercury's "classy people can be whores" comment "makes you wonder whether 'Killer Queen' is really a displaced self-portrait").

THE CONTEXT **37**

"Killer Queen" reached #2 in the UK and #12 in the US. Its success was mirrored by that of *Sheer Heart Attack*, released November 1 in the UK, November 12 in the US, reaching the same positions as the single in both countries. It was a supremely confident album: Brian showing off his guitar skills (and tape delay effects) on "Brighton Rock" and concisely capturing the spirit of the band's first US tour on "Now I'm Here," Freddie, by turns majestic ("In the Lap of the Gods") and playful ("Bring Back That Leroy Brown"), Roger again celebrating the rock 'n' roll lifestyle ("Tenement Funster"), and John coming up with his first composition ("Misfire"). There was even support among the normally curmudgeonly press, with *NME*'s Tony Stewart calling it "the most important rock album of the year—a grand accolade for the much-maligned Queen."

Queen at London's Rainbow Theatre, November 20, 1974. This show was added to the itinerary after the first show sold out.

THE CONTEXT

THE ROCK 'N' ROLLER:
Roger Taylor

Freddie Mercury may have been Queen's resident dandy, but it was Roger Taylor who epitomized the band's rock 'n' roll spirit—both on and off stage.

Roger Meddows Taylor was born on July 26, 1949, in King's Lynn, Norfolk, where he lived with his parents, Michael and Winifred, until he was four. After the birth of his sister Clare, the family moved to Truro in Cornwall. Like Brian May, Roger's musical ambitions were inspired by Lonnie Donegan. After seeing Donegan perform on TV, Roger promptly learned to play the ukulele and started a schoolboy skiffle group, the Bubblingover Boys, though he later recalled their efforts as "dreadful!"

As rock 'n' roll took off, Roger moved to guitar. But he ultimately proved to have an even greater affinity for the drums. He first played on a used snare drum, then received a new snare and cymbal for Christmas in 1961, eventually working up to a full kit. His next band, the Cousin Jacks (later Beat Unlimited), was another group of school friends. He then joined a more professional group, Johnny Quale and the Reactions, later simply the Reactions (plural) and then The Reaction (singular). The band played covers of artists they liked: Elvis Presley, Ray Charles, the Rolling Stones, and, as musical tastes changed over the decade, Jimi Hendrix and Cream. The band's members came and went, with Roger later becoming the singer, moving his drum kit down front. His distinctive raspy voice was instantly recognizable, but he was also capable of hitting the high notes, a useful skill in building Queen's signature harmonies. As a drummer, he favored a hard-hitting style, citing Mitch Mitchell, Keith Moon, and John Bonham as influences.

> **"His favorite saying was 'I'm gonna be a pop star.'"**
> —GEOFF DANIEL, BANDMATE IN THE REACTION

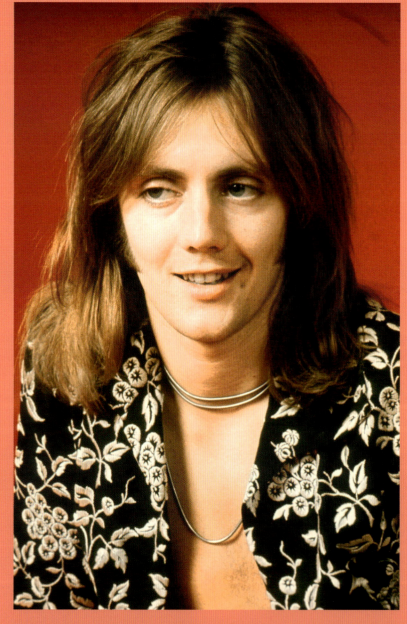

Roger Taylor—Queen's resident party boy.

(TOP) **A very youthful Roger with his first serious band The Reaction. Roger played drums and later became the band's singer.**

(ABOVE) **Roger on tour in 1976, a year which saw the band play the US, UK, Australia, and their beloved Tokyo.**

The Reaction got a chance to record in the spring of 1966 when Quale tapped the band to back him while he recorded a demo at a makeshift studio set up at an old cinema. Quale recorded four songs, and The Reaction was allowed to record two songs on their own: Wilson Pickett's "In the Midnight Hour" and James Brown's "I Got You (I Feel Good)." The tracks weren't meant for commercial release, but it was a chance to gain a little experience.

"His favorite saying was 'I'm gonna be a pop star,'" fellow band member Geoff Daniel remembered of Roger. "He said it all the time and it used to drive everyone mad." But when he headed off to the London School of Medicine to study dentistry in the fall of 1967, Roger promised his parents he'd leave his drum kit behind and focus on his studies. During the next year's summer break, he got The Reaction going again, whetting his appetite to pursue music. When he returned to London in the fall of 1968, and his friend tipped him off about the "Musicians Wanted" ad posted at Imperial College, he was well ready to join Brian in Smile. As he said later, "Really, I moved to London to be in a group."

He became the most fashion-conscious member of Queen and the kind of long-haired Lothario most likely to have an attractive woman (or two) on his arm. Songs like "Modern Times Rock 'n' Roll" and "Tenement Funster" enshrined his rock 'n' roll persona, but his greatest songwriting success for Queen came with "Radio Ga Ga," a paean to the glory days of radio that was not only a worldwide hit but also added an impromptu bit of audience interaction at the band's concerts, when crowds began mimicking the handclaps seen in the song's video. "These Are the Days of Our Lives," from *Innuendo* (though jointly credited to Queen, the song was mainly written by Roger), was a poignant look back at the band's early years.

In 1977, Roger became the first member of Queen to release a solo record, issuing the single "I Wanna Testify" (a cover of the Parliaments' song) with his own "Turn on the TV" on the flip side. He's had the most side projects of any Queen member, having released five solo albums, and, once it seemed clear Queen wouldn't be touring after 1986, forming the band The Cross, who were together until 1993, releasing three albums along the way. Conceding these outside projects never attained Queen-like sales, he told *Mojo* "I make my solo records mainly for fun."

Roger also put in guest appearances over the years, providing drums and/or backing vocals on records by Elton John, Taylor Hawkins, Kansas, Roger Daltrey, and Gary Numan, among others. Among his many honors, in 2020, Roger became an Officer of the Order of the British Empire (OBE), making him the second member of Queen to receive a royal honor.

These days, Roger's live appearances are usually alongside Brian May, representing the Queen brand. And he still conveys the impression of being on the lookout for a good time. As he once observed, "I always felt it was my job to enjoy myself"—and it's a job he's succeeded at immensely.

QUEEN'S STAR WAS in steady ascent, as Chris Welch noted in *Melody Maker*: "And step aside all ye who scoff or mock, for Queen are trundling ahead with inexorable momentum." A headlining UK tour in the fall was followed by an eight-day European tour (including two shows that saw the band terribly mismatched with US Southern rockers Lynyrd Skynyrd as an opening act). On February 5, 1975, they began their first headlining US tour in Columbus, Ohio. It was deemed a success, though a number of dates had to be canceled due to problems Freddie had with his throat. After a break, an eight-date tour of Japan began on April 19, where Queen were received rapturously; the country would quickly become one of their favorite destinations.

But trouble was brewing at home. Despite their increasing success, the band didn't feel they were being properly compensated, only being paid a paltry £60 a week by Trident. In his defense, Norman Sheffield, in his book *Life on Two Legs*, contended that the band were still in debt to Trident. The company had invested well over £200,000 in Queen, on everything from instruments to costumes to lighting equipment to touring expenses. He assured them larger paydays were coming but that royalties were only paid out a few times a year.

That wasn't enough to mollify the band, who decided to break with Trident. They promptly hired a lawyer, Henry James "Jim" Beach, and went shopping for a new manager. They worked briefly with Don Arden (who'd worked with Small Faces and Electric Light Orchestra), then considered Led Zeppelin's Peter Grant, turning him down because Grant wanted them to sign to Zeppelin's Swan Song Records. Eventually, they were referred to John Reid, Elton John's manager. Reid, "blown away" by Queen's live performance, agreed to take them on.

Confident they now had the right person looking after their business interests, Queen could finally give their full attention to making their next record. As Reid put it to his new charges, "OK, lads, I'll take care of your worries, I'll get you out of debt. You just go away and make the best album you've ever made."

Queen was ready to rise to the challenge.

Queen in the Netherlands on December 9, 1974, a day after playing the Congresgebouw in The Hague.

2

The Sessions

"We just thought that we would go out, not restrict ourselves with any barriers, and just do exactly what we want to do."

—FREDDIE MERCURY,
MELODY MAKER, NOVEMBER 1975

(PREVIOUS) **Queen in London, August 1975**, a few months before they'd release their own mix of rock and opera.

(TOP) **Rockfield Studios in Wales,** where much of *A Night at the Opera* was recorded.

(RIGHT) **The bucolic Ridge Farm,** where Queen held extensive rehearsals for *A Night at the Opera*.

(OPPOSITE) **London's Olympic Studios** was one of six studios Queen used to record their fourth album.

SO HOW DO YOU go about making the best album you've ever made?

For Queen, it meant journeying to Ridge Farm Studio, outside Rusper, Sussex, for an intensive period of rehearsal in July 1975 (lasting three or six weeks, depending on the source). The band enjoyed the rural setting. "There was very much a family atmosphere. It was all very informal with flared trousers, or in the case of Freddie, very short shorts and black-painted fingernails," Frank Andrews, the farm's co-owner, recalled. "They played snooker and tennis—Freddie was really good at tennis. Or they went for swims in the pool. They also loved our dog and were constantly playing with it." A reporter and photographer from the Japanese magazine *Music Life* were also on hand doing a story on Queen, taking pictures showing the band relaxing in the verdant grounds, playing tennis, hanging out beside the pool, and rehearsing; Freddie was photographed playing a white Bechstein piano had that been rented for him to use during the sessions. The magazine also wrote brief pen portraits of the band members, with Brian described as "very considerate of others," Roger "the most mischievous and bubbly member," how John "always has a smile on his face," and that Freddie "exudes dignity and majesty."

The band then moved on to Wales, settling in at Rockfield Studios, located outside the town of Rockfield in Monmouthshire, where part of *Sheer Heart Attack* had also been recorded. The former farm had been converted into a studio by two brothers, Kingsley and Charles Ward, in 1963. Dave Edmunds was the first artist to find success with a song recorded at Rockfield ("I Hear You Knocking" in 1970), and subsequent acts that worked there included the Flamin' Groovies, Hawkwind, Budgie, and Motörhead. It was one of a total of six studios Queen would use while recording the album, the others being Sarm Studios, Roundhouse Studios, Olympic Studios, Scorpio Sound, and Lansdowne Studios, all London-based.

What turned out to be *Opera*'s last track had already been recorded before the 1975 sessions began. On October 27, 1974, Brian and Roger had recorded Brian's arrangement of the British national anthem, "God Save the Queen," at Trident. It was a tradition for British theaters to play the anthem at the end of an evening's entertainment; now a younger audience had their own rock-influenced version. The recording was played for the first time just a few days later, at end of the band's October 30 show in Manchester, and has been the standard closing number at Queen's concerts ever since. There was another session at Trident in July 1975—their last session at the studio, as it turned out— to record a new version of "Keep Yourself Alive" for a proposed US single. But Elektra ended up reissuing the *Queen* album version as a single instead (the re-recording remained in the vaults until it was included as a bonus track on the 2011 reissue of *Opera*).

Now it was time to tackle the recording of their fourth album.

"What always happened when we went to record an album was that we all brought in our ideas and plunked them on the table," Brian said in the making-of documentary *Inside the Rhapsody*. "And from that, some would get thrown out, some would get developed, new ones would come in. And gradually there was a feeling of what kind of atmosphere on the album we were aiming for." On *Opera*, the majority of the tracks would be by Mercury, who composed five songs, with May right behind him, writing four. Taylor and Deacon wrote one song each.

A tape box from Rockfield dated August 18, 1975, established when the sessions began. The band's ingenuity in the studio was taken to a new level. As Roy Thomas Baker, again in the coproducer's chair, explained to *Sound on Sound*, it was "the summit of everything we were doing before recording and mixing became automated." He was speaking about "Bohemian Rhapsody" in particular, but he could just as well have been referring to the album as a whole.

Brian at London's Hammersmith Odeon during the tour promoting *A Night at the Opera*, November 29, 1975.

THE PRODUCER:
Roy Thomas Baker

Along with the band members themselves, there was one other person who played an important role in helping Queen develop their sound: producer Roy Thomas Baker.

Roy was born on November 10, 1946, in London, two months after Freddie Mercury's birth. The fact that he was around the same age as Queen's members helped make their relationship one of equal standing; there was no "generation gap" such as there was between the Beatles and their producer, George Martin, who was fourteen years older than the eldest Beatles, Ringo Starr and John Lennon.

His first job, at age fourteen, was working for Decca Records, starting out as a tea boy and eventually moving up to engineer. While employed by Decca, he worked with the D'Oyly Carte Opera Company, an experience that would later serve him well when working on Queen's more extravagant productions. After a stint at Morgan Studio, he moved on to Trident, where he "basically handled all the stuff no one else could cope with." By the time he met Queen, Roy had engineered or produced records by T. Rex, Free, Nazareth, and Gasolin'.

Following *A Night at the Opera*, Baker coproduced *A Day at the Races* with Queen. The two then took a break from each other. In the wake of his success with Queen, Baker relocated to the US, where he produced the first four albums by the Cars. The arrival of punk rock made him consider a new approach to his work, wanting to get a sound that was "a bit more sparse." Even so, he couldn't escape the influence of his former band entirely. "When I did the first Cars record, we purposely did it very sparse," he told *Mix*, "but when the harmony vocals come in, there are as many vocals there as there were in a Queen record. The only difference is it was in and then it was gone. 'Good Times Roll' is a classic one for that . . . I was able to put big vocals on a sparse, punkish background, sort of inventing post-punk pop."

In 1977, Roy returned to work with Queen on their most eclectic album, *Jazz*. He went on to become senior vice president of A&R at Elektra Records, and over the years, he's produced a wide variety of artists, including Cheap Trick, Devo, Alice Cooper, Ozzy Osbourne, Mötley Crüe, The Darkness, T'Pau, and the Smashing Pumpkins.

(LEFT) Two-thirds of Queen with producer Roy Thomas Baker at a press conference in New Orleans on October 31, 1978; the band would host one of their most notorious parties later that evening.

(OPPOSITE TOP) Roy Thomas Baker, seen here at LA studio The Village in 2005, had worked with the D'Oyly Carte Opera Company early in his career, good training for his later work with Queen.

50   QUEEN AND A NIGHT AT THE OPERA

"My whole thing is, the more different you can sound from anything else around but still be commercially successful is great!" he told *Mix*. "Over the years, I've always hearkened back to that philosophy. People need an identifiable sound. When your song is being played on the radio, people should hear who that is, even without the DJ mentioning who it is. If you don't have that identifiable sound, you are getting merged in. If the DJ isn't mentioning who it is, then nobody will know who it is. It will just be another band, and nothing is worse than being anonymous. That is exactly what you don't want."

The collaborations between Queen and Roy resulted in an immediately identifiable sound, making the band and the producer anything but anonymous.

"Roy brought great perfectionism and a flawless technical approach."

—BRIAN MAY ON ROY THOMAS BAKER

THE SESSIONS   51

People speculated endlessly about the meaning of Freddie Mercury's songs, but he generally denied there was anything personal about them.

As with Queen's previous albums, both band and producer were eager to experiment. For Mercury's vocal on "Lazing on a Sunday Afternoon," he was recorded singing in the studio, with the vocal then sent from the recording console to a pair of headphones inside a bucket, with a mic placed inside the bucket to capture the sound. The result was what Baker described as a "megaphone effect," making the final track sound like a 78-rpm record playing on an old-time gramophone.

Other tracks were more time-consuming, such as "Love of My Life," one of Freddie's most enduring ballads. Though often said to be about Mary Austin, John Reid revealed to authors Matt Richards and Mark Langthorne that Freddie told him the song was about record executive David Minns, the man he had his first serious relationship with. It's an explanation that makes more sense, given that the song's narrator is beseeching

QUEEN AND A NIGHT AT THE OPERA

his love to not leave him, which was not the dynamic of the Mercury/Austin relationship. Publicly, Mercury denied the song was about anyone: "I simply made it up. There's nothing personal about it."

An otherwise simple band arrangement became complicated when Brian agreed to play harp on the track (Freddie: "I'm going to force him to play 'til his fingers drop off"), which he found challenging, as he'd never played the instrument before. He ended up recording the part chord by chord, though he told *On the Record*, "Actually, it took longer to tune the thing than to play it. It was a nightmare because every time someone opened the door, the temperature would change and the whole thing would go out. I would hate to have to play a harp on stage." But he felt the start-and-stop process was worth it in the end: "[It] actually worked out quite nicely, because we were able to position the arpeggios all across the stereo [mix], as you can hear in that introduction."

Brian was equally precise in creating the "horn" parts on the bittersweet "Good Company." The sounds of a clarinet, trumpet, trombone, and another instrument he described as "a sort of extra thing, I don't really know what it was supposed to be, on top," were all done by him on four different guitars, with the trumpet and trombone parts recorded one note at a time. "Very painstaking but a lot of fun because it had never been done before," he explained in the *Classic Tracks* episode that focused on the making of *Opera*. "I don't think I would do it these days unless there was a very good reason!"

It was typical of Brian's methodical approach to his work. "He was completely meticulous, note by note," engineer Gary Langan told *Mojo*. "If he was doing guitar parts there were certain things that he could hear that I couldn't. Invariably, he'd be absolutely right. If he was working on what we'd call a guitar orchestra, he'd have a big picture already there." Brian also used a small amp that Deacon had made, which gave his guitar more of a "horn" sound.

Freddie's vaudevillian romp "Seaside Rendezvous" had Freddie and Roger recreating woodwind and brass instruments with their voices. As Freddie boasted to a reporter, "We don't believe in having any session men, we do everything ourselves, from the high falsetto to the low bassy *farts*, it is all *us*."

Brian's epic "The Prophet's Song" was another complicated number with its varying sections: heavy, churning rock, an a cappella vocal sequence, and a blistering guitar solo. "It was a terrible struggle to convert what was in my head into real music," Brian told *Uncut* about the song, which was inspired by a dream he'd had when the band was making *Queen II* that had left phrases like "people of the earth" (the song's original title) going around in his head. "I had different versions of the riff, and I couldn't figure out how they all fitted together, or if they even should fit together . . . I was sitting there, making myself ill, worrying that I hadn't distilled the essence of the dream, and the song would be a failure." To another interviewer, he recalled, "I remember having reams and reams of paper with little bits scribbled on them, and yards and yards of cassette material, and I didn't want to let any of the little ideas go." Mercury concurred, later telling *Record Mirror* that May "practically went insane trying to get it together."

Brian used a different tuning for the song, tuning his bottom string to D to give the guitar "a lot more depth, a real sort of doomy kind of growl to it." But the song's most remarkable element came about due to what he called his interest in "delays and the business of canon." He'd previously used his guitar in experimenting with tape delays, fascinated by the sounds created when the delayed signals met up and harmonized with each other. What would happen if you did that with vocals?

He prepared a demo for Freddie to hear, demonstrating what he had in mind; through the use of delay, Freddie would end up harmonizing with himself. The technique was similar to what's referred to as a "canon" in musical terms, wherein an initial melody is followed by an imitative melody that comes in after a specified break. In "The Prophet's Song," this sequence would last almost two and a half minutes. The delay was created by using two stereo Studer tape machines, the tape coming off the reel of the first machine, then going to the second machine for the playback, "so the tape would actually be running across the room," Baker explained. The track's opening "wind noise" was actually the sound of an air conditioner, with a phaser on the microphone. The surge in sound you hear at the 6:32 mark was achieved in postproduction, capturing the sound of the tape being started from a dead stop, "so we got the whole track to [surge] and then cut back into the mix again. That also couldn't be done on faders or pre-mix, that was a post-mix scenario," Baker said. May had a different recollection of what appears to be the same moment: "We did a mix of the piece onto quarter-inch tape. Then we played it backwards, and I varispeeded the machine at the precise moment downwards to a stop, copying onto another tape. Then we turned the result back around and spliced it (literally, with sticky tape) into the master mix. It was a tricky edit."

While "Death on Two Legs," Freddie's ruthless number aimed directly at Trident's management, wasn't as technically demanding, it did cause some emotional consternation. The song, originally called "Psycho Legs" for the fierce manner in which Mercury attacked the piano, was so lyrically vituperative that Brian felt uncomfortable about singing on it. "I think even we were a bit taken aback by how vicious Freddie wanted it to be," he said. "There's a sense of humor to it, but with Freddie there was a lot of anger there." It was also said that Freddie kept the music in his headphones so loud while recording the number that his ears started to bleed.

The brash "Sweet Lady" came about as a result of Brian's desire to write a rock song in a tempo generally used for waltzes, going from 3/4 in the verse to 4/4 in the chorus. "I think in your ear, you kind of refuse to hear it in 3/4, which is why it's still powerful I think," he said. Taylor would find the transition from verse to chorus a bit difficult to negotiate.

John's "You're My Best Friend" saw the bassist finally stepping up to the songwriting plate with a delightful slice of pop. He composed the song on an electric piano, an instrument he wanted to use on the final recording. But when Freddie declined to play the instrument ("It's tinny and horrible and I don't like them"), John learned to play the part himself. He also ensured that Taylor's drum sound departed from what May called his usual "big, fat, natural drum sound," instead making it "all very crunched up and compressed." Taylor, recognizing the song's commercial potential, didn't object.

Roger's "I'm in Love with My Car" featured another unusual time signature, 6/8, "slightly different from your average rock song," he agreed. Brian wasn't sure how seriously to take the song on first hearing the demo, asking Roger, "You are joking, aren't you?" But while the song's subject matter was decidedly tongue-in-cheek, Roger treated it with the utmost seriousness, further enlivening it with the roaring sound of his own Alfa Romeo dropped in at the song's conclusion.

Brian's "'39" took the band into the hitherto unexplored realm of skiffle, a type of folk music that became popular among aspiring young musicians in 1950s Britain. May suggested Deacon play an upright double-bass on the track, to give it the right kind of homespun atmosphere, and was pleased when his bandmate "picked up the technique in no time."

And then there was the song that would become the album's most notable track.

THE ROOTS OF "Bohemian Rhapsody" date back to Freddie's days at art college, when he first began writing songs. One number he'd written (but not completed) with fellow student Chris Smith opened with the narrator telling his mother he'd just killed a man. Thinking it had something of a Western theme, it was named "The Cowboy Song." Freddie kept tinkering with it over the years; as he put it later, the song "didn't just come out of thin air." One version of the lyrics from 1974 was entitled "Mongolian Rhapsody." When he played it on the piano for Roy Baker earlier in 1975, he'd provoked laughter when, after the opening ballad section, he interrupted his playing to announce, "Now, dears, this is where the opera section comes in." Clearly, Freddie had taken some unexpected avenues in developing the song.

There had been other Queen songs that abruptly changed musical moods, such as the sudden jump into overdrive on "Doing All Right" from their debut album. But there had been nothing like the extreme changes that came in "Bohemian Rhapsody": the opening a cappella section followed by a ballad section, which led into the opera section, which exploded into a hard rock section, then transitioned back to a ballad. In a sense, "Bohemian Rhapsody" was something of a distillation of *Queen II*'s "Side Black" down to a single song.

There were a lot of moving parts, and, with each being recorded separately, no one but Freddie had any clear idea of how they would all fit together. He had no demo to play for them, only chord sequences he'd written down in his notebook, which only he seemed able to decipher. "I remember doing one recording session in Rockfield where Freddie was saying, 'These are the notes,'" Deacon recalled in the *Magic Years* documentary, "and he goes 'dum, dum, dum, dum,' and it seemed to have no connection with anything." But if they couldn't quite grasp what the completed number would sound like, everyone trusted Mercury's direction in the studio. "Freddie had the framework in his head," Brian explained. "Then we set about embroidering it."

The backing track was recorded at Rockfield (with a thirty-second gap left for the opera section), the band playing in their standard piano/bass/drums configuration; it can be heard in its entirety in the *Inside the Rhapsody* documentary. As Brian explained while listening to the playback, the occasional error was left in due to recording on tape: "Nowadays you could get into the hard disc and start repairing things, but in these days the take was the take. Apart from a very few little things, nothing could be done to it. So you used the take. You might get the odd little glitch on the piano, whatever, but it would stay that way. That's the human way it was."

One unusual element was that the backing vocals for the hard rock section were laid down at the same time as the rest of the backing track, before the lead vocal had been recorded. "That wasn't the regular way of doing things," Baker said, "because the lead vocal would normally dictate the phrasing of the background vocals. But we wouldn't have had enough tracks left for the rich backing vocals if we hadn't gone down this route."

The London studios were used for the extensive overdubbing. Brian used different guitars to create a broad palette of different sounds: "There's a lot of colors, quite deliberately. I used a lot of different pick up settings and different amps even, to get different sounds." A variety of mics were used, from which Baker could choose and blend the different signals ("It's a technique that I still use today"). Mics were set up behind Brian's amplifiers, which were backless, "to capture some ambience and the full spectrum of the guitar sound." Echo was added to the guitar part in the ballad section to add an ethereal quality; elsewhere, mics were put down metal or concrete tubes "to get more of a honky sound." The "prrring" sound you hear on the "shivers up my spine" line was made by Brian scratching the strings behind the bridge on his guitar.

THE HOMEBUILT GUITAR:
The Red Special

Combine a chunk of mantelpiece from an old fireplace, a bar from a bicycle saddlebag holder, two motorbike valve springs, and some mother-of-pearl buttons, among other items. Let it simmer for a year and a half. And what have you got? A guitar that's unlike any other in the world.

The sound of Brian May's handmade guitar is a major element of Queen's music. It's been heard on every Queen album and is played at every concert. And the story of its meticulous creation has made it an icon in its own right.

Brian's decision to make an electric guitar was a matter of economic necessity—he couldn't afford to buy one of his own. He asked his father, an electronics engineer who was good at making things ("He made all our household appliances, including our TV," May recalled), for assistance. It was a project in which both father and son happily immersed themselves. The body was made from blockboard (softwood glued together and sandwiched between two boards of plywood) with inserts from the wood of an oak table; the finished piece was given a mahogany veneer. The neck (featuring twenty-four frets instead of the usual twenty-two) was made from a fireplace mantel, the wormwood holes filled in with wooden matchsticks. The bridge was sawn out of a block of aluminum. The tremolo arm came from a bicycle saddlebag holder capped with the tip of a knitting needle from Brian's mother's sewing kit. Just about every part of the guitar was made of repurposed materials except for the pickups, which Brian purchased at a shop in central London.

Brian and his father worked on the guitar from August 1963 to October 1964. It acquired its name, Red Special, from its reddish-brown color (May also affectionately refers to it as the "Old Lady"). He brought another personal touch to how he plays the instrument, not using a pick but a coin. After finding plastic picks "too bendy," he began looking for something with more substance. "Then one day I picked up a coin, which happened to be a sixpence, and I thought, 'That's all I need,' he told the *Guardian*. "Sixpences are very soft metal, which doesn't hurt the guitar strings, but if I turn that serrated edge at an angle to the string, I can get that kind of articulating, percussive consonant sound—I call it graunch. Before about 1950, they had a high content of nickel, which makes them really soft, so I especially like a 1947 sixpence—the year that I was born."

May has had replicas of the guitar made to be used as backups (it's a backup you see in the "We Will Rock You" and "Spread Your Wings" videos). Over the years, official replicas have also been made for sale; at the time of writing, you could buy replicas of the instrument at the "Brian May Guitars" website. Brian and Simon Bradley even wrote a book about the guitar, *Brian May's Red Special: The Story of the Home-Made Guitar That Rocked Queen and the World*, recommended for anyone who wants to get a (literal) inside look at the guitar that contributed so much in shaping Queen's sound.

> "We had no idea how big a part the Red would play in my life—I thought I'd just have fun with it at home."
>
> —BRIAN MAY, THE *GUARDIAN*, 2014

Brian's famous Red Special, which he made with his father in the 1960s and still plays today.

Instead of a guitar pick, Brian plays the red special with a coin, a British sixpence, preferably one from 1947, the year of his birth.

A fine lot of British dandies. Queen in 1976, still riding high on the success of *A Night at the Opera*.

The bass was given additional treatment as well. Baker had Deacon record his bass part three times, each recorded in a different way—direct from the bass, direct from the amp, and from a speaker in the studio—with the signals then blended together. "That was a favorite technique of Roy's who wanted to get the most out of the bass," Brian explained.

For the hard rock section, Mercury double-tracked his vocal but did it a little out of sync so that the listener could "feel the humanity of the two voices," in Brian's words. He himself played two different guitars during this section and noted that the three guitar runs he plays that begin at 4:45 are each different, something that presented a challenge when he played the song in concert. The "horn" sound on this particular passage came from using the amp Deacon had made, May pointing out that the guitar "almost sounds like a trumpet when you first hear it."

Unsurprisingly, recording the opera section was the most time consuming. "That section alone took about three weeks to record, which in 1975 was the average time spent on a whole album," said Baker. One reason it took so long is because Mercury kept adding to it; from the initial thirty-second gap, it grew to just over a minute. "When we started doing the opera section properly, it just got longer and longer, and we added more and more blank tape," Baker recalled to *Mojo*. "Every day we thought, 'It's done now,' and then Freddie would come in with another lot of lyrics and say 'I've added a few more Galileos here, dear,' and it just got bigger and bigger."

Baker and Langan gave an extensive interview about the track's recording to *Sound on Sound*, explaining that as the twenty-four tracks they had available filled up, they had to keep bouncing down tracks to free up space for more recording. "We formed a three-part harmony by recording one harmony at a time and bouncing," Baker explained. "So we did three tracks of the first part and bounced it to one track, three of the second, and three of the third. We would then double bounce to one section, so that particular phrase would have a three-part harmony just on one track. We would do this to each background vocal part across the song and ended up with fourth generation dupes on just one of the parts. By the time we mixed two of the other parts together, the first part was up to eight generations. This was before we wore out the master and began making 24-track to 24-track tape transfers." As he summarized in the same interview, "The making of 'Bohemian Rhapsody' was basically one continuous track bounce!"

The legend is that the track featured 180 vocal overdubs, which some have challenged as an exaggeration. It's possibly a misunderstanding of how its making was described, Mercury telling BBC Radio 1 they "recreated a sort of 160- to 200-piece choir effect"—not meaning they'd done 160 overdubs, but had overdubbed enough times to create the sound of 160 (or 180 or 200) voices. But there was certainly enough overdubbing to cause the tape to start wearing thin: "You could hold the tape up to the light and see through it," said May. Alarmed at losing all their hours of work, the tape was quickly transferred before everything wore away, but the repeated bounces had nonetheless eroded some of the sound quality, resulting in some harmonies that were "a little dissident," Baker admitted, "such as two notes next to each other which weren't quite spot on in passing phrases. We left those there, because they weren't classed as mistakes. In classical music they are allowable, whereas in rock music they normally are not. But in passing phrases it seems to work OK. If there was anything we heard at the time which we thought we wouldn't get away with, we would just wipe it and re-record it. So everything you hear was planned, albeit disjointedly planned, the way it should be."

When the track was finally completed and played for the first time, everyone was astounded at what they'd achieved. "It wasn't until the final day when it was all mixed and we all sat back and listened to it we realized what we'd done," Langan told Queen biographer Mark Blake. "We sat there in the control room and thought, 'Ye gods.' It was a seminal moment."

As the sessions continued, the band became increasingly excited about the album. Freddie was captured in an ebullient mood when *NME*'s Julie Webb came by Scorpio Sound in September, when the band were in the midst of overdubbing, telling her, "We've finished all the backing tracks and it's beginning to sound better than we expected." Webb watched the recording of the opera section of "Bohemian Rhapsody": "If they sang '*no no no*' once, they sang it 20 times in the space of about 10 minutes. And on each occasion someone would find fault. It must get exceedingly tedious." ("After you've done 'No, no, no, no, no' about 180 times you feel like you're in a lunatic asylum," Freddie conceded.) But on hearing the playback, Webb found it "truly magnificent, undeniably Queen yet with greater depth than on any previous efforts."

Freddie enjoyed a good rapport with Webb and ran down all the album's tracks for her, calling John's poppy "You're My Best Friend" "a lovely little ditty," Brian's "Sweet Lady" "a heavyish ditty in *stupendous* ¾," and "The Prophet's Song" "an outrageous, mammoth, epic track . . . one of our heaviest numbers to date." And he gleefully described his own taunting "Death on Two Legs" as "a nasty little number which brings out my evil streak." Overall, he relished the fact that the band were able to stretch out on *Opera*: "There were a lot of things we wanted to do on *Queen II* and *Sheer Heart Attack*, but there wasn't space enough. This time there is. Guitar-wise and on vocals we've done things we've never done before."

And the album was yet to be completed. Determined to meet their deadline of finishing before the upcoming UK tour, Mercury stated that Queen vowed "to work 'til we are legless. I'll sing until my throat is like a vulture's crotch. We haven't even reached the halfway stage yet, but from the things I can hear, we have surpassed anything we've done before musically."

Such comments served to whet the public's appetite for the album's release. But in addition to the music that had been created, Baker later pointed out the many technological advances that were unremarked upon at the time: "If we hadn't produced certain effects by hand, nobody would have bothered to invent the box that did it automatically, and I'd like to think that a lot of the stuff we were doing in the '70s started trends and got copied later by machines."

By the time work was finally completed in early November, just days before Queen headed out on tour, it was said to have cost in the region of £40,000 (over a quarter of a million dollars in today's money), which would have made it the most expensive album ever recorded at the time. But the band always denied that figure, though without revealing the actual cost.

As for the album's title, the most commonly circulated story is that the idea came when the band was at Rockfield, unwinding after a tough day in the studio by watching the Marx Brothers' *A Night at the Opera* in Baker's room. But Freddie told journalist Harry Doherty a different story at the time of the album's release, saying the name had been chosen at the end of the sessions: "It was going to be called all sorts of things, and then I said, 'Look, it's got this sort of operatic content. Let's look upon it that way.' Then Roger and I thought of the title. It fitted, not only because of the songs, but because of the high singing."

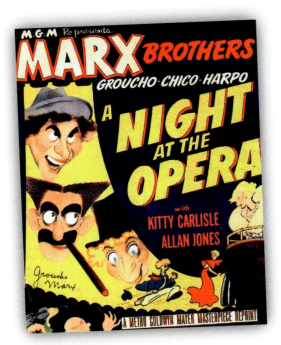

BRIAN HAS REFERRED to *A Night at the Opera* as Queen's *Sgt. Pepper's Lonely Hearts Club Band*. It's a good comparison, not only because of the differing musical styles each album contains—it's the most musically varied album of Queen's career—but also because of how each band member pushed the boundaries of the technology available at the time. The band had steadily honed their skills in the studio over the course of making their first three albums. Now, working with a sympathetic producer, they had reached a new peak and were justifiably proud of what they'd accomplished.

"It was wonderful to be able to take the time to do this stuff in the studio which I'd always dreamed of doing," Brian said in the *Classic Albums* episode. "That's the great thing about *Night at the Opera*, we had the time, we were given the opportunity to explore those avenues rather than be rushing in and out.

"And I'm sure there were a load of times when we were thinking, 'Well, you know, we're pushing this too far.' Because we were trying to push forward the band. We were trying to do things which had not been done and people would say couldn't be done."

Queen had responded to those naysayers by showing that it *could* be done. Now all that was left was to see was how the public would respond to the new album.

(ABOVE) **Though the legend is that this Marx Brothers film inspired the name of Queen's fourth album, Freddie said he and Roger thought it up independently. It fitted "not only because of the songs, but because of the high singing," he said.**

(OPPOSITE) **Freddie at the Hammersmith Odeon, London, on November 29, 1975.**

3

Side One

"TOGETHER WE'LL SAIL ACROSS THE SEA"

Death on Two Legs (Dedicated to . . .)

Lazing on a Sunday Afternoon

I'm in Love with My Car

You're My Best Friend

'39

Sweet Lady

Seaside Rendezvous

THE COVER OF *A Night at the Opera* is designed to look like a theater program. It's a plain white cover, with the band's name and album title in black cursive script and, for the first time, the Queen logo in glorious full color. The back cover is equally regal in its simplicity: the album credits and song titles, also in cursive script, in a black-bordered box with illustrations of androgynous *dramatis personae* in two corners, one in a mask, the other's face in a frozen scream, perhaps from the sword that appears to be going through their head. The graphic theme continues on the inside of the gatefold sleeve, with printed lyrics, color-tinted headshots of each band member, and a "Cast" list, which features a single touch of humor: Freddie Mercury being credited with "vocals, vocals, Bechstein Debauchery and more vocals." And, of course, the obligatory "No Synthesizers!"

Visually, it was the most sophisticated cover design the band had yet produced (some would say it was never surpassed), and it set the stage perfectly for the theatrical extravaganza that was to follow.

"DEATH ON TWO LEGS (DEDICATED TO . . .)"
(Freddie Mercury)

The piano arpeggios are heard roiling in the distance, approaching like a herd of galloping horses or the rush of the incoming tide. Then, a growing cacophony of sound arises (the distorted clanging of guitars, a bowed double bass, a percussive ratcheting), culminating in a scream from Roger, before the sonic maelstrom is suddenly cut off in midflow. It's a startling beginning to the album, leaving you a bit apprehensive as to what might come next.

Then the piano takes over again, playing as starkly as in any Bernard Herrmann film score—a possible inspiration for the song's working title of "Psycho Legs"—with equally sharp guitar interjections from Brian. And then comes Freddie's vocal.

"'Death on Two Legs' was the most vicious lyrics I ever wrote," Freddie told *Circus* magazine with some pride in 1977. Indeed, the words drip with venom throughout, Freddie's snarling vocal perfectly matching the lyrical vindictiveness. The all-out attack is further buttressed by Brian's stinging guitar lines (which were actually written by Freddie, as he'd composed the song on the piano).

The litany of insults is awe-inspiring, the object of Mercury's wrath variously depicted as a mule, a shark, a rat, an "overgrown school-boy," and "king of the sleaze" who's advised to consider suicide as an option. Though it's now well-known the song was an attack on their management, Freddie himself never mentioned Barry or Norman Sheffield's names in the lyrics or in any interviews, and you needn't know the backstory to appreciate the song. Anyone who's ever held a grudge can enjoy a good takedown of a perceived enemy.

The band goes all out after the last chorus, with Freddie, Brian, and Roger harmonizing over the pummeling music, climaxing in a final sentence sung a cappella alongside a reversed cymbal sound that brings the proceedings to a sudden end—as if being sucked into a vacuum.

(PREVIOUS) **From 1975 on, Queen's setlists would always include songs from *A Night at the Opera*.**

(OPPOSITE) **Freddie played the piano so fiercely on "Death on Two Legs" that the song was jokingly referred to as "Psycho Legs."**

"LAZING ON A SUNDAY AFTERNOON"
(Freddie Mercury)

The next four songs on the album neatly illustrate the differing artistic sensibilities of the band members.

After the rage of "Death on Two Legs," there's a quick about-face into what's surely the most delightful song that Freddie Mercury ever wrote, evincing the same kind of 1920s-era whimsy as more modern tracks like the New Vaudeville Band's "Winchester Cathedral" and the Beatles' "Honey Pie" (written by Paul McCartney, the Beatle most inclined to draw on music hall and vaudeville for inspiration). "I like to feel that I can write songs in different atmospheres," Mercury told journalist Robert Duncan. "Why not? I want to try my hand at different things because I can."

In a concise one minute and seven seconds, Freddie takes you through one week in the life of a London dandy. He's hardly the "ordinary guy" he professes to be, as becomes especially clear when he details how he spends his Fridays painting at the Lou-*vre*, Freddie decisively rolling the *R*s in the second syllable. The backing vocals add to the song's charm, in particular the bemused "There he goes again . . ." in response to the narrator's gallivanting ways. Brian provides a jaunty guitar solo as the song heads offstage, and Roger's final cymbal flourish is the cherry on top.

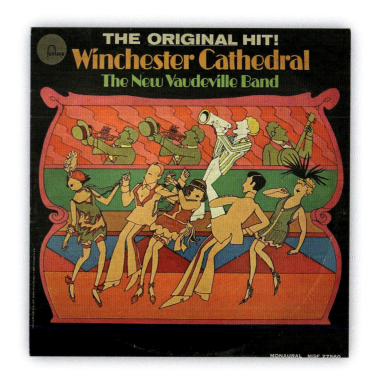

(OPPOSITE) **Brian crafted the perfect guitar line to bring "Lazing on a Sunday Afternoon" to a jaunty conclusion.**

(RIGHT) **Freddie's "Lazing on a Sunday Afternoon" had the same sense of 1920s-era whimsy as the New Vaudeville Band's hit "Winchester Cathedral."**

SIDE ONE

"I'M IN LOVE WITH MY CAR"
(Roger Taylor)

"I'm in Love with My Car" is Roger's signature song. For while he would go on to write "Radio Ga Ga," one of Queen's most memorable hits, that song features Mercury on lead vocal. This song is one-hundred percent Roger Taylor.

The use of car imagery as sexual metaphor—autoeroticism, if you will—has long been a staple of rock and R&B, from Jackie Brenston's "Rocket 88" (which some have called the first rock 'n' roll song), to Wilson Pickett's "Mustang Sally" (whose title refers to both a woman *and* a car), to the Angels' "You Can't Take My Boyfriend's Woody" (when he pops the clutch, "he'll make you think you're in reverse"), to Danielle Dax's "Cat-House" ("Got my engine throbbing and my sockets jumping"), and on and on. Roger's addition to that fine catalog is the couplet in which he dumps his girlfriend in favor of "a new 'carburettor,'" not to mention all the other references to clean machines, squealing radials, and grease guns. Freddie wasn't the only member of Queen with a penchant for innuendo.

It's the first real blast of rock on the album, turbocharged by Taylor's pounding drums and throat-shredding vocals, especially when he hits the high notes in the second verse (he also helps fill out the thick sound by playing rhythm guitar on the track). "It's very tuneful, but of course the vocal is the thing," he explained in a documentary. And though the humor of the song's premise is clearly evident, Roger plays it straight, throwing himself into the song with dead seriousness in what proves to be a punishing workout. The unusual 6/8 time signature adds to the fun, Taylor calling it "a great time signature to play in. It rolls, it has a certain unstoppable rolling quality."

The roaring exhaust you hear at the song's end comes from Roger's own Alfa Romeo, heading into the song's double ending; following initial fade-out, there's another short burst of guitar and drums, and the car revving up once again. The liner notes say the song is "Dedicated to Johnathan Harris, boy racer to the end"—Harris, one of the band's roadies, owned a Triumph TR4.

"I'm in Love With My Car" quickly became Roger's signature song.

A rare Yugoslavian pressing of "You're My Best Friend."

"YOU'RE MY BEST FRIEND"
(John Deacon)

After sticking his toe into the songwriting waters with the brief "Misfire" (which ran just under two minutes) on *Sheer Heart Attack*, John finally emerges as a composer with a well-polished gem of his own.

"You're My Best Friend" is the least likely song one would expect from Queen. It's nothing more than sweet, unadulterated pop, in this context providing a sharp contrast to the hard rock blast of the preceding number. Freddie also sings the song without any camp affectations; it's a love letter straight from the heart.

John wrote the song for his wife, Veronica Tetzlaff, whom he'd married earlier in 1975. But referring to his partner as a "best friend" gives it a touch of innocence and broadens its scope; it could be a song about a family member or friend as much as a romantic partner. There's also a softer musical feel to it, due to there being no "Bechstein debauchery." John had written the song on an electric piano and ended up playing it on the song himself. The instrument gives the track a buoyancy and blends well with the typically lush harmonies.

And it's the first song on the album to really make extensive use of Queen's vocal harmonies. As Brian has observed, their voices "interacted quite magically," and on this number in particular, the all-encompassing warmth of their harmonies emphasizes the song's endearing sentiments. One might think of the Beach Boys, another group known for their harmonizing prowess (and the song's theme makes it one the 1960s-era Beach Boys could have performed themselves).

The rest of Queen welcomed Deacon as a blossoming songwriter. Brian called the track a "perfect pop song." Freddie was equally effusive, telling *Record Mirror*, "John has really come into his own. Brian and myself have mostly written all the songs before, and he's been in the background; he's worked very hard, and his song's very good, isn't it?" It is.

"'39"
(Brian May)

Brian's songs often had an undercurrent of melancholy—something that was certainly true of most of his contributions to *A Night at the Opera*.

"'39" is a seemingly upbeat sailing song with an unexpected twist that you might not notice if you're not listening carefully. It's primarily an acoustic number, aside from a bit of electric guitar. With Deacon on the upright double bass, Taylor adds to the folk sound by limiting himself to playing bass drum and tambourine. As Brian takes the lead vocal, Freddie's sole contribution is as a backing vocalist (along with Roger and Brian). It's a hearty song, the kind of number that makes you want to tap your foot and sing along.

The song tells the story of a voyage, the first verse describing the ship sailing away on a lovely sunny morning, with a subtle hint of what's to come in the reference to "milky seas." In the second verse, it's revealed that the "ship" is not a seagoing vessel but a spaceship, sent out in search of new worlds for future colonization. The trip is a successful one—a new world has been found—but it's also a bittersweet triumph for the narrator. For time has passed more swiftly on Earth than in space; he's aged a year, but his wife is now an old woman (a phenomenon known as the time dilation effect). In contrast to the celebratory pulse of the music—all thumping good spirits—the lyric ends on a despairing note with the words "pity me."

It makes sense that Brian, with his interest in all things astronomical, would craft such an intriguing song about space travel. But he's said that the song also referred to his sense of displacement on returning home from his own "voyages" on the road with Queen, readjusting to day-to-day life after experiencing "this vastly different world of rock music." As he put it in one of Queen's fan-club newsletters, the space travel theme is the song's "concrete level. But on another level it's about emotional journeys, which is harder to explain and rather sadder."

Giving the song a folk arrangement makes the main character more relatable: "You can't really identify with him if you think of him as a spaceman or something in the future," May said. It's a humanizing element that gives the song both its power and its poignancy.

(OPPOSITE) **"His song's very good, isn't it?" Freddie said about John's first big hit, "You're My Best Friend." The band performs at London's Hammersmith Odeon, November 29, 1975.**

(LEFT) **Though seemingly a folk song, "'39" is gradually revealed to be a song about interplanetary travel.**

"SWEET LADY"
(Brian May)

Some would say that this is the song that mars an album that would otherwise be a complete masterpiece. Others might regard it as the track that gives the album a bit of a human touch—after all, nobody's perfect.

Either way, "Sweet Lady" is the weakest song on the album; one might even call it cheesy. The primary reason for its inclusion is seemingly because it adds to the record's rock quotient, but it pales in comparison to previous Queen rockers like "Seven Seas of Rhye" and "Now I'm Here." It feels more like filler, lacking the lyrical wit or musical inventiveness of the band's other hard rock fare (think of Brian's guitar pyrotechnics on "Brighton Rock"). That said, even a weak Queen song is better than most bands' best material, and there's more to "Sweet Lady" than is apparent at first glance.

Freddie's back on lead vocals (though he doesn't play piano). The lyrics depict a squabbling couple. In the first verse, the narrator complains about the titular lady, while in the second verse she complains about him (or her—in an interesting twist, both the narrator and the girlfriend refer to each other as a "sweet lady"). Freddie has his tongue wedged just far enough in his cheek to let you know he's not taking it all too seriously. Meanwhile, the shifting time signatures (3/4 in the verses, 4/4 in the chorus) keep the listener slightly off-balance, trying to figure out where the next beat's going to fall.

During the last minute and a half, the song unexpectedly shifts into high gear, May, Deacon, and Taylor kicking up the dust together, then, as Mercury calls out "Awww—runaway! Come on!" going into a near-frantic (the musicians never completely lose control) double-time beat. It's a giddy ending that leaves you with a smile on your face. Perhaps it's not such a bad song after all.

Brian changed up the time signatures in "Sweet Lady," which is waltz tempo (3/4 time) in the verses and 4/4 in the choruses.

SIDE ONE

"SEASIDE RENDEZVOUS"
(Freddie Mercury)

The bright piano intro lets you know straightaway that you're in for another spirited romp. And so you are; "Seaside Rendezvous" is a song of sheer joy.

The song mines the same music hall terrain as "Lazing on a Sunday Afternoon." One can imagine Freddie jauntily strutting the boards while singing the song, sporting a smart vaudevillian *ensemble*—well-tailored trousers, white shirt, bowtie, striped jacket, and a straw boater, perhaps. He's deliriously camp, lapsing into French ("*Très charmant*, my dear!"), using vintage words like "jollification," and vaulting up into falsetto voice.

The song's most remarkable element comes during the instrumental break. Foreshadowing the vocal extravaganzas to come on Side Two, Freddie and Roger vocally emulate, respectively, woodwind and brass sections, with Roger creating an especially nice "trumpet" solo at 1:05 ("We can use Roger's voice as an instrument," May noted. "It's quite incredible"). The sequence ends with the sound of tap dancing. Sources differ on whether this was created by Taylor and Mercury drumming on the studio console with thimble-capped fingers or Taylor alone tapping a washboard with thimbled fingers. Roger's description of "Bring Back That Leroy Brown" (from *Sheer Heart Attack*) is just as apt here: "Although it's kind of a novelty, it's very advanced technically. We loved having a go at those things." Unusually, May isn't featured on this track, either vocally or instrumentally, though a touch of his ukulele playing would've seemed well suited to this musical genre.

The song breezes to its conclusion with Freddie looking for a dance partner, begging his sweetheart to be his valentine, and comparing himself to that most romantic of matinee idols, Rudolph Valentino, before sailing off into the moonlight. It brings Side One—Act One, really—to a charming close. The narrative arc of the songs also makes this the more upbeat, positive side of the record, moving from the malevolence of Freddie's opening salvo, "You suck my blood like a leech," to his cheery adieu: "Give us a kiss!"

Freddie's delightful "Seaside Rendezvous" brings Side One of the album to a close with a cheery "Give us a kiss!"

Side Two

"NOTHING REALLY MATTERS"

The Prophet's Song
Love of My Life
Good Company
Bohemian Rhapsody
God Save the Queen

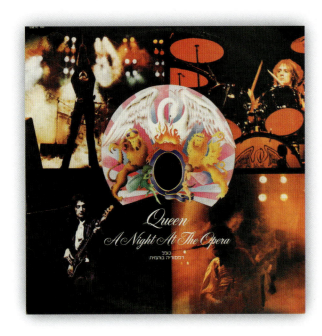

SIDE ONE MAY have its moments of aspersion. But overall, its mood is bright and positive; even the vengeful threats of the opening "Death on Two Legs" have been tempered by the time the first side ends. In stark contrast, Side Two treads darker territory. Apocalyptic visions. Unrequited love. A wasted life. Existential dread. Truly, Side Two is *A Night at the Opera*'s Side Black.

(PREVIOUS) ***Opera*'s Side Two culminates with Queen's best-known song, "Bohemian Rhapsody."**

(ABOVE) **An Israeli pressing of *A Night at the Opera*.**

(OPPOSITE) **Brian has admitted he's felt that "Bohemian Rhapsody" has overshadowed his own equally elaborate "The Prophet's Song."**

"THE PROPHET'S SONG"
(Brian May)

The first sound you hear is that of the wind, bringing with it the kind of chill that makes you wrap your coat around yourself more tightly. Then an acoustic guitar, accented by the plucked strings of a toy koto (a smaller version of the full-sized Japanese stringed instrument). Brian had received it as a gift during Queen's tour of Japan earlier in the year and wanted to feature its "beautiful evocative sound" on the track. There's great delicacy in this section that can be best appreciated by listening to the song on headphones.

"The Prophet's Song" holds the distinction of being Queen's longest number, running eight minutes and twenty-one seconds (or at least their longest *song*; the untitled instrumental piece that's the last track on the 1995 *Made in Heaven* album runs twenty-two minutes and thirty-two seconds). And were it not for "Bohemian Rhapsody," "The Prophet's Song" would likely have been regarded as *Opera*'s cornerstone track. May has admitted he's felt that the success of "Bohemian Rhapsody" overshadowed his own equally elaborate creation. But having it open Side Two (Act Two, if you're thinking theatrically) gives it a more prominent position in the album's running order.

The song is a warning, a prophecy of doom if humanity doesn't change its ways. "A feeling that runs through a lot of the songs I write is that if there is a direction to mankind, it ought to be a coming together," Brian told *Melody Maker* at the time of the album's release, "and at the moment it doesn't seem to be happening very well." The powerful music matches the forcefulness of the seer's predictions; this is a man you *will* listen to. The fanciful characters that populated Queen's earlier numbers—the Fairy Kings, Black Queens, and "quaere fellows"—all had a touch of whimsical sparkle. Not so here. This prophet is deadly serious.

"Bohemian Rhapsody" has its operatic section; "The Prophet's Song" has a vocal canon. It's one of Freddie's most extraordinary performances, and again, it's one that needs to be listened to through headphones to truly appreciate, as his first vocal is placed in the center of the mix, followed by the second on the left, and then third on right, meaning that eventually you're surrounded by Mercury's voice on all sides. It gives you a sense of what May wanted to do with the track; when the song was later given a 5.1 mix, he spoke enthusiastically of how "you can hear it all, swirling around and churning in three dimensions. It's pretty much how I always dreamed that track would sound."

Following Freddie's vocal workout, the rest of the band comes storming back in, Brian firing off salvos on his guitar like thunderbolts. The Prophet's final words echo the rallying cry of the 1960s that love is all you need. And then the vision fades in a crash of cymbal and the sound of the wind rising once again.

(OPPOSITE) **Though a challenging song, Queen did manage to perform "The Prophet's Song" live.**

(RIGHT) **"The Prophet's Song" features one of Freddie's most extraordinary vocal performances—one that needs to be listened to through headphones to be truly appreciated.**

"LOVE OF MY LIFE"
(Freddie Mercury)

There's a lovely segue as the blowing wind of "The Prophet's Song" dissipates and the notes of the acoustic guitar (accented by the toy koto) lead directly into the piano introduction to one of Freddie's most beautiful ballads. His piano playing clearly reveals the influence of classical music on his own compositions. Yet Brian has said that Freddie doubted his skills as a pianist, which over time led to his playing the instrument less often and bringing in someone else in to play the parts. Thankfully, that isn't the case here. Freddie's playing becomes an extension of his inner heart, his emotions translated into musical poetry.

The minimal instrumentation at the beginning—he sings the first verse accompanied only by his own piano—also highlights how beautiful his voice could be. Slowly, slowly, the rest of the band come in. Vocal harmonies emphasize particular passages ("all my love," "bring it back"). Brian chimes in with a baroque guitar solo during the bridge, hitting a high note as Freddie plays faster notes beneath him on the piano, finally climaxing in a burst of the orchestral guitars that are so much a part of Queen's sound. The harp, heard most prominently before the first verse and at the song's conclusion, adds another classical touch.

It's a song of heartbreak, a song of loss. Freddie pleads for his love to return and even imagines a time when that's happened, when past conflicts are all "by the way," and the pair have been reunited in everlasting bliss. But then real life intrudes once again, and we're left with Freddie's final plea, his passionate desperation set against gorgeous banks of backing harmonies. It's here that the harp comes in again, bringing the song to a close with an exquisite flourish.

(OPPOSITE) **Brian said that Freddie doubted his skills as a pianist, which over time led to bringing in someone else to play the parts. Thankfully, that isn't the case with "Love of My Life."**

"GOOD COMPANY"
(Brian May)

This is the third song (along with "Lazing on a Sunday Afternoon" and "Seaside Rendezvous") that conjures up an earlier musical era, opening with the sounds of a vintage jazz band. It's the music of another age being recreated with a modern sensibility, à la The Temperance Seven, a British band who had hits in the 1960s with the songs "You're Driving Me Crazy" and "Pasadena." Brian, an admitted "absolute addict" of the band, recreates their sound using only his guitar—a most impressive feat.

Then comes the brisk strum of a ukulele, played in the style of George Formby, a British musician who became a star in 1930s and '40s wartime Britain and another of Brian's favorite performers (May later bought one of Formby's ukuleles for £70,000 at auction). Both elements, the jazz band and the ukulele, create a cheerful and sunny mood. But the lyrics paint a different picture.

It's Brian's second lead vocal on the album. He relates an initially prosaic tale about growing up, marrying the girl next door, and settling into a seemingly comfortable life. Then things take a downward turn. The marriage becomes insular, an "institution" that's more akin to a prison, the couple eventually so isolated from each other, the narrator admits he "hardly noticed" when the relationship fell apart. Now he's left alone, wondering about the meaning of his "life's insanity," with his father's advice about keeping good companions around you still ringing in his ears. May later noted it was a similar kind of approach that George Formby would take, "telling quite moving stories in a very lighthearted musical way."

Taken as a whole, the song is a sober, even somber, reflection on the emptiness of a materialistic life—and one coincidentally released on an album that would open the door to bringing the band's members all the wealth they'd ever dreamed of. It's also perhaps a strangely downbeat song to come from a young man who'd just turned twenty-eight, with so much of life to look forward to.

"I kind of imagined myself at the age I am now," he said in explaining the song in an interview with the author in 2023. "I imagined what it would be like to be looking back at all this stuff and what would have been important in my life; what was lost, what opportunities were seized, and what went by. I was just trying to get an overview of what life was about and imagining myself as some old, old geezer in his armchair looking back on his life."

And there's a final discordant touch. After the song is apparently over, you hear a multitracked guitar "trill," wavering between B minor and C# minor, bringing the song to an unresolved, and unsettling, ending.

(OPPOSITE FAR LEFT) **"Good Company"** is the sound of a different era, influenced heavily by the British retro jazz outfit The Temperance Seven, whom Brian adored.

(RIGHT) **Brian ends "Good Company"** with discordant multitracked guitars, creating an unsettling end to the song.

"BOHEMIAN RHAPSODY"
(Freddie Mercury)

Is this the real life?

It's a song that may feel overfamiliar now, having been heard as a hit on the radio, then on classic radio, in television shows and films, and, unfortunately, too many commercials. But it is without question Queen's most extraordinary song.

The opening lines are sung a cappella, the gorgeous harmonies of May, Mercury, and Taylor soon to be accompanied by Mercury's piano. The song becomes a ballad, with a dramatic narrative about murder; Freddie's highly emotional vocals are alternately confessional and despairing. The rest of the band have come in instrumentally by now, the sequence climaxing with an equally dramatic guitar solo from Brian.

And then comes a sudden change of mood.

"It was just something that I'd wanted to do for a long while actually," Freddie told UK music weekly *Sounds* about the song's opera section. "And it needed a lot of thought. I did a bit of research, y'know, but I still wanted it to be very much a Queen thing. I wasn't trying to say it was the authentic opera or whatever, I just wanted it to be opera in the rock 'n' roll sense."

Meaning, it was meant to be fun, a bit of levity following the song's more serious beginnings. The lyrics are peppered with words that are alternately playful (it's not "silhouette" but "silhouetto") and ominous (Beelzebub, the name of a demon), not to mention the high-pitched "Galileos." Freddie's rough drafts of the song also featured words like "matador" and "belladonna." It's a sequence that's extravagant and over the top yet lighthearted as well; never meant to be as intimidating as classical opera, it's delivered with a wink.

Nor does it overstay its welcome. After a little more than a minute, the song virtually explodes into hard rock. It's the kind of high-energy rock turn Queen excelled at, with Freddie now singing forcefully of how he won't be abused and Brian navigating the guitar runs he found tricky to master when playing the song live ("I always kind of fought [with them] on stage"). And then the song glides back to earth, sliding into the ballad tempo of the opening, concluding, with almost wistful despondence, "Any way the wind blows . . .," followed by the shimmering sound of a gong.

Surely such an elaborate, carefully crafted song must be saying something of monumental importance. But Freddie, who rarely discussed the meaning of his songs, played down the idea that "Bohemian Rhapsody" had any deeper meaning at all, telling *Sounds*, "I'm going to shatter some illusions: It was just one of those pieces I wrote for the album." It was not an answer that was going to satisfy most people.

Some interpret the song literally as the story of a condemned man awaiting trial, sentence, and execution. Others see it as a "coming out" song about Freddie's coming to terms with his sexuality. Jim Hutton, Freddie's boyfriend during his final years, told biographer Lesley-Ann Jones, "It was about how different his life could have been, how much happier he might have been, had he just been able to be himself, the whole of his life."

But publicly, Freddie never said much more than "People should just listen to it, think about it, and then decide what it means." "I do think Freddie enjoyed the fact there were so many interpretations of the lyrics," Brian told Mark Blake, adding, "I think it's best to leave it with a question mark in the air." And so the meaning of Queen's most famous song remains something of a mystery.

(OPPOSITE) **A selection of "Bohemian Rhapsody" seven-inch picture sleeves attests to the song's far-flung popularity. Top row: Portugal, Türkiye, United Kingdom (limited-edition blue vinyl); Middle row: France, Denmark, Belgium; Bottom row: Germany, Japan, United Kingdom (purple vinyl).**

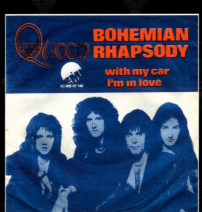

MAMA MIA!
The Landmark Video

Though Queen prided themselves on being thoroughly up to date in both their music and appearance, it was a forty-year-old photograph that provided the inspiration for their most memorable video.

Photographer Mick Rock met the band in 1974, when they were planning the cover for *Queen II*. "They wanted to be totally fabulous," Rock recalled to *Mojo*. "They had a sense of their own destiny." With the album sides called "Side White" and "Side Black" instead of the usual "Side One" and "Side Two," the band wanted to carry over this theme to the album cover (which would be a gatefold sleeve). Most of the band wanted the outer cover to be white. But Freddie and Rock held out for black, and they got their way, "which, as it turned out, was an amazingly fortunate decision," Rock observed.

Rock had come across an image he thought would work perfectly for the front cover. It was a photograph of Marlene Dietrich from the 1932 film *Shanghai Express*. In the black-and-white shot, Dietrich's expression is neutral as she looks upward, her hands at her chin, a cigarette drooping from her left hand with a smoldering inch of ash. Surrounded by a black background, her head appears to be floating in midair. Rock recognized that the picture had the same air of glamour that Queen wanted to convey. "I saw the connection immediately," he told biographer Lesley-Ann Jones. "It was one of those visceral, intuitive things. Very strong. Very clear. Glamorous, mysterious, and classic. I would transpose it into a four-headed monster. They had to go for it." Freddie instantly grasped what Rock wanted to do. "I shall be Marlene," he told the photographer. "What a delicious thought!"

The final cover shot had the four band members' heads in a diamond formation, looking somber, their eyes in shadow, Freddie crossing his arms over his chest. Twenty months after *Queen II*'s release, the image became the starting point for the "Bohemian Rhapsody" promo clip. Queen were busy rehearsing for their UK tour but took time out on the evening of November 10, 1975, to shoot the clip at their rehearsal venue, Elstree Studios, working with director Bruce Gowers, who'd directed the 1974 *Live at the Rainbow* concert film for the band.

The band wanted to make a promo clip, as they felt they couldn't mime to such a complex song on a program like *Top of the Pops* (*TOTP*). Which makes it ironic that the clip itself is relatively simple. It primarily shows the band in performance, along with some minimal special effects, intercut with sequences of the band emulating the *Queen II* cover (even Deacon is seen miming, though he never sang on the band's albums—and note that he's wearing a Queen T-shirt). The band worked quickly, completing filming in four hours, and were able to sit down with Gowers at the local pub before closing time. Depending on the source, the final cost was said to be either £3,500 or £4,500.

It was a bargain at either price. The band first viewed the clip on November 19 while on the way to Cardiff for their show that evening, stopping off at a television studio in Harlech to watch. "The general consensus was quite good for four hours [work], with much laughter during the operetta," noted a reporter from *Sounds*. The clip debuted on *TOTP* the next evening. As the single headed for the top of the charts, an "enhanced" version of the clip was devised, featuring a wall of fire superimposed over the beginning and ending, known as the "flames version;" perhaps it was felt it might be too monotonous to watch the same clip week after week and some variation was needed. But the clip's distinctiveness made it compulsively rewatchable—and ripe for parody. Plugging "parodies of Bohemian Rhapsody video" into an online search engine will bring up numerous iterations, featuring cats, the Muppets, *Star Wars* characters, a "Menopause Rhapsody," and, in response to the COVID-19 pandemic, "Coronavirus Rhapsody."

"Bohemian Rhapsody" was far from being the first music video. From the early days of motion pictures, musical acts were featured in short films showing them in performance. The Beatles were likely the first big act to use such clips more extensively as a promotional tool and even varied the format—the clips for both "Penny Lane" and "Strawberry Fields Forever" don't show the group performing and feature no miming at all, something unusual in a clip even today. In the case of "Bohemian Rhapsody" (which was shot on video, not film), the single's success is seen as being tied inextricably to the excitement generated by the video, a type of cross-promotion that would become standard when MTV began broadcasting in 1981.

And it remains one of Queen's most popular creations. In 2019, *Billboard* announced that "Bohemian Rhapsody" had reached one billion views on YouTube. What else can one say but "Mama Mia!"

> "A good video can make all the difference."
> —BRIAN MAY

(ABOVE) **Queen's groundbreaking video for "Bohemian Rhapsody" took inspiration from Mick Rock's sleeve photograph for 1974's** *Queen II* **album, which did double duty here on the Italian picture sleeve for the single.**

(RIGHT) **For the 1974 photo shoot, Mick Rock had taken inspiration from an iconic image of Marlene Dietrich in** *Shanghai Express*.

"GOD SAVE THE QUEEN"
(Traditional, arr. Brian May)

What better number to bring the evening to a close than this rock-infused version of the British national anthem? It was the standard closing number played at every respectable theater at the end of a performance, with the audience expected to stand and not leave until the anthem had concluded. Brian's guitar work is naturally the main attraction here, with Roger also acquitting himself nicely, bookending the piece with an introductory snare drum roll and, at the end, a flourish of tympani. It's the consummate ending to this most theatrical of Queen's albums.

(OPPOSITE) **Brian's guitar work is the main attraction of the band's take on the British national anthem, which provides a fittingly theatrical ending.**

5

The Release and Tour

"*Night at the Opera* is really the conundrum, because I don't really think of it as a very commercial album. But it was the one that broke all the records."

—BRIAN MAY,
MELODY MAKER, SEPTEMBER 1976

(PREVIOUS) **Freddie onstage at the Bournemouth Winter Gardens during the *A Night at the Opera* tour on December 4, 1975. By the end of the year, both the album and the "Bohemian Rhapsody" single would top the UK charts.**

BACK TO THE EVENING of *A Night at the Opera*'s preview in November 1975. After hanging around their manager's office until they were assured that the tapes of the album had been delivered, Freddie, Roger, and John (Brian being too tired to attend) finally headed off to Roundhouse Studios, greeted on arrival by a placard reading "Welcome to *A Night at the Opera*." The playback went smoothly, though Freddie took it upon himself to berate the attendees when they didn't provide sufficient deference as "God Save the Queen" was played, shouting, "Stand up, you cunts!"

Afterward, the group went out to dinner. "Thank goodness that's over," Freddie sighed to *Melody Maker*'s Harry Doherty in the car on the way to the restaurant. During the meal, he spoke enthusiastically about the record: "It's going to be our best album. It really is." But the next day, Queen went back into the studio to put a few more finishing touches on it.

By the time of the album preview, "Bohemian Rhapsody" had already been released as a single, though not without some difficulty. Conventional wisdom at the band's record label was that no radio station would play a song that ran to nearly six minutes. When John Reid played the song for his other big client, Elton John, his reaction was one of astonishment. "You're not actually going to release that, are you?" Elton said to his manager. "For one thing, it's about three hours long. For another, it's the campest thing I've ever heard in my life. And the title's absolutely ridiculous as well."

The record company's view was that the track would have to be edited. The band considered it, going so far as to have a proposed edit prepared by simply cutting the opera and hard rock sections. But the edit clearly gutted the song, and ultimately the band held firm—the song would have to be released at its original length. As Freddie told *Phonograph Record* a few months later, "We said, you'll release it or else, figuring it was out of the ordinary, has a lot to say, and if it did click would really put us on the map."

The story then becomes a bit muddled. The most common version is that the band passed on an advance copy to Kenny Everett, a DJ at London's Capital Radio, telling him not to play it, though delivered with a wink communicating that that's exactly what they wanted him to do (other variations have Everett taking a copy surreptitiously without the band's knowledge or being given a copy by a non-band member). Everett then played the track on the radio over the weekend of October 11 and 12 (either four or fourteen times, depending on the account), prompting a strong enough response from listeners that EMI's hand was forced, and they agreed to release the full song as a single.

Queen's fan-club newsletter, released the same month, noted that "Bohemian Rhapsody" was planned for single release on October 28 (the usual release date cited is October 31), suggesting that the newsletter could have been prepared after Everett played the song on the radio. "Diddy" David Hamilton, a DJ on the BBC's Radio 1, later argued to Mercury biographer Lesley-Ann Jones that it was his playing the song that made "Bohemian Rhapsody" a national hit, because Capital Radio only broadcast to London.

In any case, the single entered the UK chart at #47. Reviews were inevitably mixed. *NME* cautiously observed, "It's performed extremely well, but more in terms of production than anything else." Freddie was impatient with such attitudes, telling *Melody Maker*, "A lot of people have slammed 'Bohemian Rhapsody' but you listen to that single, who can you compare it to? Tell me one group that's done an operatic single? I can't think of anybody."

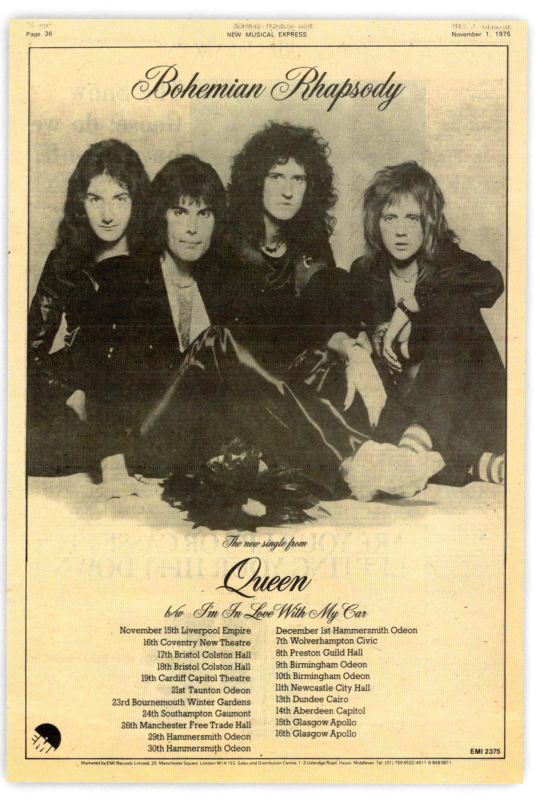

(TOP) **Capital Radio DJ Kenny Everett helped break the "Bohemian Rhapsody" single in the UK.**

(ABOVE) **EMI had not wanted to release "Bohemian Rhapsody" as a single due to its length; songs nearly six minutes long aren't often played on the radio.**

THE RELEASE AND TOUR 97

ACTION! VIDEO VANGUARDS:
The First Promo Films

Queen created some notable promotional films over the course of their career (later called "videos" when they were shot on video tape): the iconic clip for "Bohemian Rhapsody"; "Radio Ga Ga," which drew on imagery from the classic silent film *Metropolis*; "I Want to Break Free," which ruffled American sensibilities when the band members performed in drag. But their earlier efforts were a lot more basic.

Their first such clip was a production the band actually had nothing to do with. The UK television music show *The Old Grey Whistle Test* had received a white label promo copy of the band's debut album, but without any identifying information, so no one knew who the group was. The show's producer, Mike Appleton, nonetheless decided to put together a promo clip to the song "Keep Yourself Alive," syncing it with random stock footage from the vaults. Once the clip aired, EMI contacted the show's staff, and it was announced who the mysterious group was. It was Queen's first national television exposure—audio only, as the band members themselves didn't appear in the clip.

Queen would make their own proper promo films soon after, shooting clips for "Keep Yourself Alive" and "Liar" on August 9, 1973, working with director Mike Mansfield. Both films show the influence Freddie had on sprucing up the band's visual appeal. Most serious bands in the early 1970s dressed down, wearing T-shirts and jeans, often taking to the stage in the same clothing they'd worn all day. Freddie would have none of that of course, preferring outfits in all white or all black, and using upscale fabrics like crushed velvet or satin. It created a more refined look, one that would be fully on display in both songs.

Freddie is the obvious focal point throughout, especially in "Keep Yourself Alive," where he's in white (including his platform boots), his loose jacket patterned with a design of leaves. The others are all in black, though Taylor catches one's eye by wearing a sleeveless shirt with a white pattern on the front. A costume change was in order for "Liar," with Freddie now in black trousers and a black and white top that left his right arm bare, and Brian wearing a black jacket with a silver pattern. Deacon is also seen singing along on backing vocals, though he didn't sing on the actual recording.

But Queen was unhappy with the final result. The band had performed on a low stage with a white backdrop with colors projected on it, and a neon-colored filter was also used for Freddie's closeups; Queen wanting something far moodier. As a result, neither clip was officially released at the time ("Liar" later appeared on the *Box of Flix* VHS set released in 1991).

So a few months later, on October 1, the band entered Shepperton Studios in nearby Surrey to reshoot, this time with Trident's Barry Sheffield directing. The band exudes much greater confidence on this outing. In "Keep Yourself Alive," Freddie wears a black outfit, with a glittering belt at his waist, a black jacket with silver embroidery, and a black necklace; note the way he delicately brushes his hair out of his face at the end of the first verse. "Liar" has the more dynamic opening, cutting between Taylor's drumming and the other band members' handclaps. Everyone opts for black this time, Freddie in a black sequined top open to his chest (the better to display his dangling black necklace), what looks like a chain-mail brace around his right wrist, and black satin trousers with a metallic belt; Brian wearing an elaborate gold necklace and loose jacket with flared sleeves; John in shiny trousers and a black top and jacket with silver accents; and Roger in another sleeveless spangly top.

Freddie is the most animated of the four, but even he is more restrained in these later versions of the songs. Instead of extravagant movements and visual effects, the band sells the numbers through the strength of their performance; it's pure unadulterated Queen. Both clips can be found on the *Greatest Video Hits 1* DVD, released in 2002.

The promo films reveal the characteristics that would come to identify each band member: Mercury's flamboyance; May's attention to detail as he turns out another exquisite guitar solo; the solid, steady dependability of Deacon; Taylor, the band's playful party boy. Four diverse personalities that balanced each other out perfectly. The films also show the band's understanding of making a visual, as well as a musical, impact. At Freddie's instigation, the band would eventually work with designers like Wendy de Smet, Natasha Korniloff, and Zandra Rhodes, wearing increasingly elaborate creations—though only Freddie would ever wear a leotard.

> **"It's a piece of entertainment. As simple as that."**
> —ROGER TAYLOR ON QUEEN'S VIDEOS, 2021

Due to Freddie's fashion sense, Queen eschewed the *de rigueur* '70s look of T-shirts and denim jeans in favor of crushed velvet and satin.

Queen's promo films highlighted the four very different personalities that made up the band.

Boosted by the promo film shown on *Top of the Pops*, it reached the top of the chart by the end of the month, where it remained for a total of nine weeks, the longest stay of a single at #1 since 1957, when Slim Whitman's "Rose Marie" topped the chart for eleven weeks. The band learned they'd gotten their first #1 single on December 14 while on the bus headed to their gig that night in Aberdeen, Scotland. The reaction was what you'd expect, according to Roger: "We celebrated with enormous amounts of drink."

There had been another last-minute issue with the album when Norman Sheffield got wind of the lyrics of "Death on Two Legs." He immediately recognized that the song was directed at him and filed suit against EMI and the band. All parties decided to settle so as not to hold up the album's release. In addition to recouping monies already spent, Trident would continue to receive a percentage of Queen's publishing and record royalties until all such rights finally reverted to the band.

A Night at the Opera was released on November 21 in the UK, reaching #1 by the end of December. By then, Queen was the hottest act in the country. Their entire UK tour was sold out. Originally scheduled to open on November 15 in Liverpool, ticket demand (prices ranging from £1 to £2.50) was such that an additional date was added to the front end of the itinerary, meaning the tour made its debut on November 14 in the same city. That left the band even less time to prepare (Mercury told one journalist they only had two days to rehearse), and as a result, the set list featured only three songs from their upcoming album.

Kenny Everett prepared a brief introduction for the show, a recording with the sounds of an orchestra tuning up, a conductor's baton smartly tapping a music stand, and then Everett himself announcing, "Ladies and gentlemen—a night at the opera!" This was followed by a short recorded excerpt of "Ogre Battle" (from *Queen II*), leading into the recording of the opera section of "Bohemian Rhapsody," culminating in Queen themselves finally taking the stage ("in a blast of flares and white smoke" according to one review) to perform the rock section of the song, which then segued back into "Ogre Battle." It set a pattern for the future, for Queen would never perform "Bohemian Rhapsody" in its entirety. On this tour, after appearing in the opening sequence, the song would later resurface as part of a medley with "Killer Queen" and "The March of the Black Queen." In subsequent years, though the song would be presented from start to finish, the group would never attempt to perform the opera section live, leaving the stage while a recording of that section was played. "That operatic section has very often been a light show or a video show in our concerts—and I would rather have it that way than stumble through it and do something which is nothing like the record," May later explained to the *Guardian*.

The only other *Opera* songs performed during the tour were "Sweet Lady" and "The Prophet's Song." The former was more boisterous live than on record, though the time signature changes continued to give Roger some trouble. On opening night, even Freddie admitted, "I'm not sure of the words myself." As for "The Prophet's Song," Mercury felt the band didn't always pull off *Opera*'s second-most ambitious number live, telling *Record Mirror* its performance on the band's first night in Bristol was "a mere skeleton of what it should be."

But the crowd response was universally ecstatic. "Freddie's voice is in amazing good shape," wrote *Record Mirror*. "Brian's playing is just heavenly and the rhythm department is everything one would expect of it—and more." In *Sounds*, Jonh Ingham wrote of the Cardiff show, "Freddie's movements explode in perfect unison with the music, the lights and surroundings go crazy, and the audience goes berserk." He also captured their

Freddie never publicly admitted that "Death on the Two Legs" was about Trident's Norman Sheffield. But Sheffield took legal action nonetheless, which was quickly settled so *A Night at the Opera* could be released.

Queen during the triumphant *A Night at the Opera* tour at London's Hammersmith Odeon, November 29, 1975.

THE RELEASE AND TOUR 105

(ABOVE RIGHT) *A Night at the Opera* comes to New York; Queen at Big Apple's Beacon Theatre in February 1976.

(OPPOSITE ALL) When Queen toured the US in 1976, a promoter called them "the biggest act since the Beatles, absolutely the biggest since Led Zeppelin." Freddie, Brian, and John during the band's four-night stand at New York City's Beacon Theatre, February 1976.

determination: "All four have immense desire to be successful, and that kind of ambition will keep them slogging until they achieve it." Even when things went awry, they acted like pros. When performing at the Apollo Theatre in Glasgow on December 15, Mercury fell off Taylor's drum platform onto the stage; ever the trouper, he merely flashed a grin at the audience and carried on.

By the end of the year, *Opera* had joined "Bohemian Rhapsody" at the top of the charts, staying at #1 for two weeks, dropping down to #2 for a week, then recapturing the top spot for two further weeks. Tony Stewart was fulsome in his praise in *NME*: "Throughout the album they assert their individual songwriting abilities and musicianship to devastating effect" (aside from "Sweet Lady," which he described as "mutton dressed as lamb, probably the most awful rock number they've ever recorded") and hailed "Bohemian Rhapsody" as "the quintessential example of Queen's magnificence in terms of writing and production." In *Sounds*, Phil Sutcliffe called it "the meisterwerk, the magnum opus even." The album's success also spurred sales of their back catalog; all of the band's previous albums reentered the UK Top 20.

Due to demand, a Christmas Eve show was scheduled for December 24, after which Queen could finally take a break. It had been a remarkable year, and Queen could look back with pride at their substantial accomplishments. Even the ever-critical media momentarily capitulated. *Melody Maker* named them "Band of the Year," while *NME* stated, "This band are the best thing to have happened to British music this decade." Now they were ready to take on the rest of the world.

QUEEN BEGAN the new year with Freddie picking up an Ivor Novello award for "Bohemian Rhapsody." The band would spend the first months of 1976 on the road, kicking off their US tour on January 27 in Waterbury, Connecticut. Both "Bohemian Rhapsody" and *A Night at the Opera* had been released in the US in December and, though charting lower compared with the UK (peaking at #9 and #4, respectively), were nonetheless the highest charting records the band had so far released in the States. As in the UK, an enterprising DJ, Paul Drew, affiliated with the RKO radio network, had helped break "Bohemian Rhapsody" in the US after hearing it while on a visit to London. "He managed to get a copy of the tape and started to play it in the States, which forced the hand of Queen's USA label, Elektra," Roy Thomas Baker recalled. "It was a strange situation where radio on both sides of the Atlantic was breaking a record that the record companies said would never get any airplay!"

There was much anticipation for the tour. When Queen arrived in Boston, the show's promoter hailed them as "the biggest act since the Beatles, absolutely the biggest since Led Zeppelin." Most shows sold out ("the SRO crowds are ecstatic," wrote *Phonographic Record*), and a fourth date was added in New York due to ticket demand. While in the Big Apple, Freddie, Brian, and Roger enjoyed a reunion with Mott the Hoople's Ian Hunter, who was recording his solo album, *All American Alien Boy*, at Electric Lady Studios. The three Queen members, undoubtedly enjoying a *frisson* of excitement at being at the studio once owned by Jimi Hendrix and built to his specifications, provided backing vocals on "You Nearly Did Me In."

THE RELEASE AND TOUR

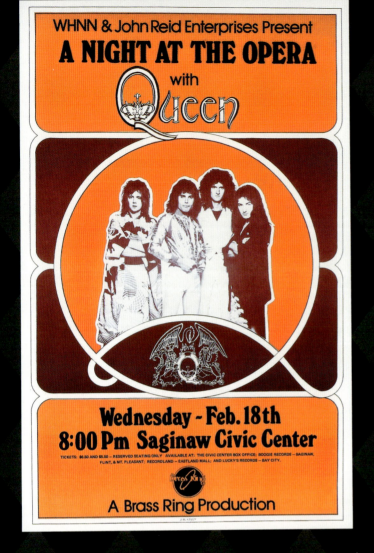
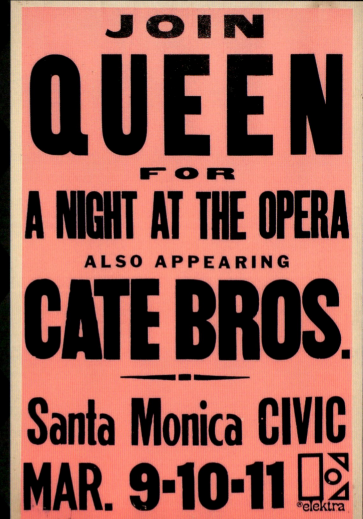

The set list was largely the same as on the previous UK tour. Another *Opera* track, "Lazing on a Sunday Afternoon," was added but ended up being dropped fairly soon due to a less-than-enthusiastic response (not to mention the song being too brief to make much of an impression during a loud rock show). And typically for Queen, despite the positive crowd reaction, the reviews were often mixed. The *New York Times* called the band "too often calculated and precious. . . . And for all the skill and invention elsewhere, the music sounds hollow at the core." Conversely, when the band played four shows at the Santa Monica Civic Auditorium, the *Los Angeles Times* called them "a group with the power, ambition and, crucially, the swagger to be a superstar attraction."

Throughout the tour, Freddie stressed in interviews that now that the band had broken through, they were keen to broaden their audience. "We just want to make sure that we appeal to as wide a cross-section as possible," he told writer Mitchell Cohen, "and not cater to just a fragment of people. It's limitless; we want to hit everyone. We've become sophisticated and disciplined and more listenable as a band, and I think we've matured and so has the audience. But I don't think we've lost the hardcore fans." For Queen, there would always be new horizons to conquer.

The US leg concluded on March 12 at the San Diego Sports Arena. Ten days later, the Japanese tour began, with the band performing eleven shows through April 4. "It's good to be back," Brian said at the opening show at Tokyo's Nippon Budokan. "It's been too long. We've been away too long." The band loved being able to perform for some of their most devoted fans once again, with Freddie announcing during a show in Nagoya, "May you all drink champagne tomorrow for breakfast." But doing two performances in one day, as happened in Fukuoka and Osaka, put a noticeable strain on his voice, and after this tour, Queen limited themselves to one show a day. The tour was originally scheduled to end on April 3 in Sendai, but ticket demand led to an additional show in Tokyo (this time at Nichidai Kodo).

The tour then moved on to Australia, with Queen returning in triumph, Freddie's vow that on their next visit to the country they'd be "the biggest band in the world" having come true beyond even his wildest expectations. As had happened elsewhere, the tour was extended. Opening on April 11 in Perth, and consisting of five shows, demand had increased the dates to a total of eight shows in five different cities, with shows added in Adelaide, Sydney, and Melbourne.

After the final date in Brisbane on April 23, Queen took a much-needed break. A second (and final) single from *Opera* was released: "You're My Best Friend" in May in the US and June in the UK. It reached #16 and #7, respectively. Queen didn't rest for long though, beginning rehearsals at Ridge Farm in preparation for recording their next album, which would also feature the title of a Marx Brothers' film: *A Day at the Races*. Sessions began in July at the Manor Studio in Kidlington, Oxfordshire, with the band ultimately working in four different studios.

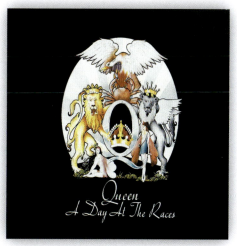

(TOP) **"You're My Best Friend" was Queen's first hit single written by John; there would be more to come. This Belgian picture sleeve is from 1976.**

(ABOVE) **The cover of *A Day at the Races* was variation of the *A Night at the Opera* cover.**

OPERATIC:
The Legendary Performances

Queen's rising popularity on their fall 1975 UK tour saw a few shows added to the itinerary, culminating with a special Christmas Eve performance at London's Hammersmith Odeon, which was broadcast live on the UK music television program *The Old Grey Whistle Test*.

The set opened with a literal bang, flash pots exploding as the band launched into "Now I'm Here." Freddie was resplendent in a Wendy de Smet–designed tight white satin suit open at the front, baring his chest, with flared "wings" at his wrists and ankles (in reference to the winged feet of the god Mercury). He offered up a "special Christmas toast" with a glass of "champagne" (according to roadie Peter Hince, he actually filled such glasses with water, not wanting to drink an effervescent beverage while he was singing). Later he changed into a tight black satin suit with equally bare chest, then had a third costume change during the first encore, coming onstage in a kimono, which he stripped off during "Big Spender" to reveal a loose white shirt and tight white satin shorts, as balloons and soap bubbles cascaded over the audience.

The band played an abbreviated set list to fit the program's time slot, but even so, the second encore wasn't filmed or broadcast. And though the crowd response had been enthusiastic, the band still felt it wasn't one of their better performances. Roger had been ill, and the rest of the band were tired after the recent touring. More importantly, they didn't like the lack of control over the final product. "It's not up to you anymore. It's up to the cameras, the lighting people," Freddie told *Sounds*' Jonh Ingham. "It's also very hard to decide what audience to cater for. The people in front of you have paid money to see you but at the same time you're doing a prestigious concert and you have to try to make sure you come across on TV." He also disliked having to shorten the show. "We were used to pacing ourselves for an hour and a half. I wouldn't want to do live TV again. Film is much better because you have control over it."

The show was rebroadcast on December 28 and then aired on BBC Radio 1 on February 28, 1976. Accordingly, it became one of Queen's most highly bootlegged shows. An official release finally came in 2015, when *A Night at the*

Dry ice and flashpots—pyrotechnics were very much a part of a Queen show.

> "They are, how you say, a great little band."
>
> —HARRY DOHERTY, *MELODY MAKER*, SEPTEMBER 1976

Odeon was released on CD, DVD/Blu-ray, and in a box set, a fitting tribute to a show that had capped a triumphant year.

The following year, Queen decided to thank their UK fans for their loyal support by putting on a free show in London's Hyde Park on September 18, 1976. Coincidentally, it was the sixth anniversary of Jimi Hendrix's death, and an indication of how much things had changed for the band. Freddie and Roger had closed their stall at Kensington Market as a sign of respect when they'd learned of Hendrix's death. Now, six years later, they were preparing to perform for their largest audience to date.

In the run-up to the concert, the band did some warmup shows, two in Edinburgh and one in Cardiff. The London show drew a crowd estimated to be as many as two hundred thousand people. Queen waited until after sunset to start their set (the show's pyrotechnics couldn't be fully appreciated in daylight). The set began with an excerpt of the instrumental that would open the not-yet-released *A Day at the Races*, which the band were in the midst of recording. They also previewed another track from the album, the ballad "You Take My Breath Away."

Freddie strode onstage in a white boiler suit (akin to what the Droogs wore in the film *A Clockwork Orange*), swiftly changing into one of his trademark bare-chested leotards (white). "Welcome to our picnic by the Serpentine!" Freddie called out after the opening numbers. "You all look very beautiful, I must say." The quotient of *Opera* songs was boosted by the addition of "You're My Best Friend" and "'39," the latter of which would later inspire the band to feature an acoustic segment in their shows.

As the show ran late, the planned encore was canceled, with police threatening to arrest the band if they returned to the stage. (Freddie later quipped he didn't wish to go to jail while wearing a leotard.) The concert was filmed, and over the years, short clips have been broadcast and turned up in documentaries, but the performance has never been released in its entirety. The reason given from the Queen camp is that the overall quality isn't good enough, leaving the curious to seek it out on the collector's circuit.

The concert was a high point in Queen's career; in *Melody Maker*'s words, the band "played a magnificent set that emphasized their status as this year's major band." "I think that Hyde Park was one of the most significant gigs in our career," Brian later said. "There was a great affection because we'd kind of made it in a lot of countries by that time, but England was still, you know—we weren't really sure if we were really acceptable here. So it was a wonderful feeling to come back and see that crowd and get that response."

(TOP) **Queen's Hyde Park concert on September 18, 1976, was meant as a "thank you" to their British fans for their support.**

(BOTTOM) **On September 18, 1970, Roger and Freddie closed their clothing stall for the day when they learned of Jimi Hendrix's death. Six years later they were playing their largest show to date at Hyde Park.**

THE RELEASE AND TOUR

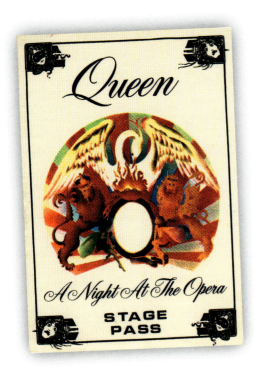

Queen now took on the role of sole producers themselves, dispensing with Baker's services for the moment (while bringing along their favored engineer, Mike Stone). *Races* was seen as a companion piece to *Opera*. Brian later stated that the two albums should have been released together ("I regard the two albums are completely parallel"), though that would surely have stunted *Opera*'s impact. "I thought it reeked of sequel" was Roy Thomas Baker's less flattering observation, and the albums' similarities did go beyond their titles. In contrast to *Opera*'s white cover, *Races* was black and featured a more decorative rendition of the band's logo. There were *Races* songs as ornate as *Opera*'s baroque flights of fancy, such as "The Millionaire Waltz" (inspired by John Reid), where Freddie briefly emulates Marlene Dietrich in his vocals. They even dabbled in foreign tongues, with Brian's "Teo Torriatte (Let Us Cling Together)," a tribute to the band's ardent following in Japan, partially sung in Japanese.

But there was also a feeling of the album being too elaborate, of going too over the top. In contrast to the breeziness of *Opera*'s "Seaside Rendezvous," *Races*' "Good Old-Fashioned Lover Boy" feels overdone; "You Take My Breath Away," *Races*' counterpart to "Love of My Life," sounds somewhat forced. Nonetheless, it reached #1 in the UK and #5 in the US and spawned a classic single in the gospel-influenced "Somebody to Love," which just missed giving Queen another UK chart-topper, peaking at #2 and reaching #5 in the US. (The subsequent singles, Brian's barnstorming "Tie Your Mother Down" and "Good Old-Fashioned Lover Boy," off an EP, fared less well; unsurprisingly, "Teo Torriatte" was also released as a single in Japan.)

Queen took time out from recording to perform a few UK shows, appearing in Edinburgh, Scotland, on September 1 and 2, and Cardiff, Wales, on September 10. They then gave a special free concert in London's Hyde Park on September 18 (coincidentally, the sixth anniversary of Jimi Hendrix's death) as a means of thanking their British fans for their support.

Work on *A Day at the Races* was completed by November; the album was released the following month. On January 13, 1977, Queen's US tour was set to begin, after which they'd head back into the studio to record their sixth album. The band was now on the album-tour-album-tour treadmill. All the hard work they'd done had brought them the success they wanted for so long—and the realization that it takes just as much hard work to keep that success going.

One of the immediate perks was the change in their living situations. No longer stuck on a minimal retainer of £60 a week, the band members quickly moved into more upscale homes. For Freddie, it also meant ending his relationship with Mary Austin. In her account, he told her he thought he was bisexual; she responded that she thought he was gay. The two hugged, then parted. Freddie was already seeing record executive David Minns, the inspiration for "Love of My Life" and the object of his affections in "Good Old-Fashioned Lover Boy." But he would maintain a close friendship with Austin throughout his life and, remembering his reliance on her during Queen's lean early years, would see to it that she was always taken care of financially.

"I'm staggered by the past year," Brian told *Melody Maker* at the time of the Hyde Park concert. "I'm amazed. I suppose now we're conscious of having to live up to something, whereas before we weren't, so that's an additional strain. I will be happy as long as I feel that we do live up to people's opinion of us.

"We're certainly not resting on our laurels in any way," he added. "We're always pushing on to new things." So it would prove. With *A Night at the Opera*, the Queen juggernaut had finally been fully launched, and the group's busiest days were still to come.

Whether in leotards or the shortest of shorts, Freddie's outfits always commanded attention.

> "I'm staggered by the past year. I'm amazed. I suppose now we're conscious of having to live up to something, whereas before we weren't, so that's an additional strain."
>
> —BRIAN MAY, *MELODY MAKER*, 1976

Queen at Cardiff Castle on September 10, 1976, one of four UK dates they played during the recording of *A Day at the Races*.

(OPPOSITE) **"Just a minute, dearies!"** Freddie introducing the band's next song during Queen's appearance in Cardiff.

Queen at Cardiff Castle, one of four UK dates they played during the recording of *A Day at the Races*.

6

Sales and Awards

"It took off like a rocket."

—BRIAN MAY, ON THE SUCCESS OF
A NIGHT AT THE OPERA

QUEEN'S BESTSELLING RELEASES then and now continue to be *A Night at the Opera* and "Bohemian Rhapsody."

The album was Queen's first to top the UK charts, also reaching #1 in Australia, the Netherlands, Finland, and New Zealand. It reached the Top 10 in seven other countries, including the US, where it peaked at #4. It has certified worldwide sales of over 6 million—half of those in the US (in comparison, both *News of the World* [1977] and *The Game* [1980], each sold 4 million copies in the US; *Greatest Hits* [1981] sold 9 million in the US). Note that prior to the arrival of Soundscan in the US and Canada in March 1991, record sales were reported by select music stores and vendors, so to some extent, sales figures prior to that date were estimates; actual sales were likely to have been higher.

"Bohemian Rhapsody" was their first single to top the UK charts, going to #1 in five other countries as well. It reached the Top 10 in seven other countries, including the US, where it peaked at #9 in *Billboard* (in *Cashbox* it peaked slightly higher, reaching No. 6). Its certified worldwide sales run to over 5.6 million, 1 million of that in the US. It's Queen's only US single to receive diamond certification (sales of 10 million) for digital sales.

The album's second single, "You're My Best Friend," reached #16 in *Billboard* (#9 in *Cashbox*), #7 in the UK, and reaching the Top 10 in three other countries. It sold over one million copies in the US—not bad for what was only John Deacon's second song.

A multitude of silver, gold, and platinum record awards would soon be heading the band's way. But the first award they received was a more personal one from their manager, John Reid. It was a solid-gold brooch, made by Cartier, that read "Queen Number 1." Each band member received one, with their name etched on the back, though Freddie's was misspelled as "Freddy Mercury."

Over the course of the next half century, accolades for the album and its first single have continued to arrive in a steady stream. On May 11, 1976, Freddie received his first Ivor Novello award, a prestigious honor named after Welsh entertainer Ivor Novello, when "Bohemian Rhapsody" won for Best Selling British Record. (It's often mistakenly written that "Killer Queen" won the Ivor Novello for Best Pop Song, but it lost out to Carl Douglas's "Kung Fu Fighting.") On October 18, 1977, both "Bohemian Rhapsody" and Procol Harum jointly received the British Phonographic Industry's BRIT Award for "The Best British Pop Single 1952–1977." On July 26, 1978, when EMI Records received the Queen's Award to Industry for export achievement, they pressed a special edition of the single on blue vinyl to commemorate the honor in a limited edition run of two hundred hand-numbered copies, making it among the rarest of Queen's records.

Reissues of "Bohemian Rhapsody" in the wake of Mercury's death, and the use of the song in the 1992 film *Wayne's World*, spurred further sales—and awards. In May 1992, the single won an Ivor Novello for "Best Selling 'A' Side." The video for *Wayne's World*, a mash-up of the movie's footage with Queen's original video, won the MTV Video Music Award for Best Video from a Film in September 1992.

(PREVIOUS) **After *A Night at the Opera*'s success, Queen became a sales juggernaut.**

(LEFT) **"Bohemian Rhapsody" has been issued a number of times in various formats. The blue vinyl version is one of the rarest, pressed in a limited edition to commemorate EMI Records receiving the Queen's Award to Industry for export achievement in 1978.**

(OPPOSITE) **Receiving another raft of awards for *A Night at the Opera* at London's Ambassadeurs Club on September 8, 1976.**

PARTY ON: *Wayne's World*

It became an iconic moment in one of the biggest comedies of 1992—and showed how the appeal of Queen's music spanned generations.

The film *Wayne's World* was based on a recurring sketch on the US comedy show *Saturday Night Live* (*SNL*), though the character (played by Mike Myers) had made his first appearance on the 1987 Canadian television variety show *It's Only Rock & Roll* in a segment entitled "Wayne's Power Minute." In the *SNL* sketches (with the first one airing on February 18, 1989), Wayne Campbell and his nerdy pal Garth Algar (Dana Carvey) cohost a public-access television show called *Wayne's World* (broadcast from the basement of his parents' home), featuring the two discussing their love of hard rock/heavy metal bands and their perennial search for "babes." The sketch quickly became a favorite and introduced a few catchphrases into the public lexicon, such as "Party on, Wayne!" and "We're not worthy!"

In the opening sequence of the *Wayne's World* film, Wayne pops in a tape of Queen's song while riding around in a car with Garth and their friends. The tape starts at the opera section, everyone lustily singing along, then doubling over in a ferocious bout of headbanging when the hard rock section begins. It's a scene that resonates because it takes you back to your own teenage years when you drove around with your friends doing the same thing.

It certainly reflected what Myers listened to as a teenager, which is why he wanted to use the song in the film (which he cowrote). By 1991, when the film was made, Queen hadn't been a hit act in the US for a decade. The film's director, Penelope Spheeris, thought the song was an "odd choice because if you are headbangers that wouldn't be your first choice to slam to in the car when you're cruising." Producer Lorne Michaels suggested they use a song by the currently hot Guns N' Roses instead. But Myers was insistent. As he told *Rolling Stone*, "At one point I said to everybody, 'I'm out. I don't want to make this movie if it's not "Bohemian Rhapsody."'" So "Bohemian Rhapsody" it was. Ironically, he seemed to regret that choice when shooting the scene. The hours the actors spent headbanging left them all with sore necks and headaches. Myers was also worried that the sequence wasn't funny. "I guarantee you it's funny," Spheeris reassured him.

Brian May contended that prior to the film's release, Myers sent him a copy of the film to show to Freddie, who, according to May, "loved it. He just laughed and thought it was great." Penelope Spheeris is skeptical of this account, saying in one interview that the timeframe between Mercury's death and the completion of the film wouldn't have made this possible: "It's really hard to believe that somebody had access to a VHS and brought it and showed it to him." Then again, if anyone could get their hands on an early cut of the film, the film's star and cowriter would be a likely contender.

Wayne's World was an instant smash, eventually bringing in over $183 million at the box office. The soundtrack, *Wayne's World: Music from the Motion Picture* (which featured "Bohemian Rhapsody"), was also successful, topping the US chart and selling over two million copies. And the video made to promote the film, which mixed footage from the movie and Queen's original promo, won Best Video from a Film at the 1992 MTV Music Video Awards. It's gone on to be considered one of the best sequences in any rock movie.

"That scene is the epitome of youthful exuberance" is how Spheeris aptly described it. "I think people that are that age love to feel that way, and people that are older love to remember how that felt and people that are younger, they want to feel that way." In short, it's a scene tailor-made for rock fans—particularly Queen fans.

> ## "I think we'll go with a little 'Bohemian Rhapsody,' gentlemen?"
>
> —WAYNE CAMPBELL,
> WHILE CRUISING IN HIS CAR WITH FRIENDS

(LEFT) **Party on, Wayne!** *Wayne's World* introduced a new generation to "Bohemian Rhapsody."

(BELOW) *Wayne's World* director Penelope Spheeris working with the cast. Star Mike Myers worried that the scene of the guys headbanging to "Bohemian Rhapsody" wasn't funny enough. "I guarantee you it's funny," Spheeris told him.

SALES AND AWARDS 125

At the time of its initial release, "Bohemian Rhapsody" was nominated for Grammys for Best Pop Vocal Performance by a Duo, Group, or Chorus and Best Arrangement for Voices (Duo, Group, or Chorus). It lost out to, respectively, Chicago's "If You Leave Me Now" and the Starland Vocal Band's ode to daytime copulation, "Afternoon Delight." But vindication arrived in the twenty-first century, when the song was inducted into the Grammy Hall of Fame in 2004. That same year, it also made the Rock and Roll Hall of Fame's "500 Songs That Shaped Rock and Roll" list, and it regularly turns up in a variety of "Best of" listings.

In addition to awards for specific songs and albums, Queen has also been recognized for their overall musical legacy, much of which, of course, can be attributed to the success of *A Night at the Opera*. Happily, a number of these honors were given prior to Mercury's death; they were not simply "legacy" awards for a band past their prime. In 1984, the Nordoff Robbins UK music charity gave the band its Silver Clef Award for Outstanding Contribution to British Music. In 1987, the band received the Ivor Novello award for Outstanding Contribution to British Music; in 2005, the band received another Ivor Novello for Outstanding Song Collection. Freddie's last public appearance was when Queen received a BRIT Award for Outstanding Contribution to Music in 1990.

(RIGHT) **Freddie's mother, Jer Bulsara, made a surprise on-stage appearance when Queen was inducted into the Rock & Roll Hall of Fame in 2001.**

(OPPOSITE) **Roger and Brian at the ceremony unveiling Queen's star on the Hollywood Walk of Fame on October 18, 2002; the star is located at 6356 Hollywood Boulevard.**

In 1992, Freddie was given a posthumous BRIT for his own Outstanding Contribution to Music. The same ceremony saw "These Are the Days of Our Lives" (paired with "Bohemian Rhapsody" on a newly released single) receive a BRIT for Best British Single. The band was inducted into the Rock and Roll Hall of Fame in 2001, received a star on Hollywood's Walk of Fame in 2002 (located at 6356 Hollywood Boulevard), and became the first band, as opposed to an individual, inducted into the Songwriters Hall of Fame in 2003. In 2004, the band were inducted into the UK Music Hall of Fame. At the 2011 MTV Europe Music Awards, they received the Global Icon Award. In 2018, perhaps to compensate for never receiving a Grammy award for any of their songs or albums, Queen were given a Grammy Lifetime Achievement Award.

On December 11, 2018, it was announced that "Bohemian Rhapsody" had become the most-streamed song from the twentieth century, as well as the most-streamed classic rock song of all time, with 1.6 billion streams and downloads of the song and video across all major streaming services around the world. A mere seven months later, in July 2019, views of the video on YouTube alone surpassed one billion views, the oldest music video to reach that number on the platform.

Awards and honors continue to accumulate. In 2022, "Bohemian Rhapsody" was chosen by the US Library of Congress for preservation in the National Recording Registry, as a record deemed "culturally, historically, or aesthetically significant."

Even items relating to the creation of the song became notable in their own right when Mary Austin, who'd inherited the bulk of Mercury's estate, decided to have Sotheby's sell his possessions in an auction entitled *Freddie Mercury: A World of His Own*. The auction was preceded by an exhibition that ran from August 4 to September 5, 2023, drawing 140,000 people eager to see what would be going under the hammer. The items were divided into six different collections, with online auctions for three collections running August 4 to September 13, and the remaining three collections auctioned over the course of three days, from September 6 to 8. The opening September 6 auction was a festive event, with some hopeful bidders dressing as Freddie lookalikes, and auctioneers opened the proceedings by pounding out the opening percussive rhythm of "We Will Rock You" on their desks.

A draft of the lyrics for "Bohemian Rhapsody," handwritten by Freddie on British Midland Airways stationary, went for $1.7 million. His Yamaha G2 baby grand piano, which was used to compose the song's timeless melody, sold for $2.2 million, the highest price ever paid for a composer's piano. Even the silver snake bracelet he's seen wearing in the song's video sold for $898,000, one hundred times its estimated value, making it the highest price ever paid at auction for jewelry owned by a rock star. And the gold "Queen Number 1" brooch, with the "Freddy Mercury" misspelling on the back, sold for $208,000. Clearly, one needed deep pockets to be able to acquire a little piece of Queen.

Both the album and its standout single (as well as Queen themselves) will undoubtedly continue to reap honors and awards in the coming years. But what's more important than record-setting figures is the timeless appeal of the music—music that's part of a legacy that's priceless.

(OPPOSITE AND ABOVE) **The *Freddie Mercury: A World of His Own* auction, held in 2023, saw many iconic pieces being auctioned off, including the robe Freddie wore on Queen's final tour and his handwritten rough draft of the lyrics to "Bohemian Rhapsody."**

7

Queen after *A Night at the Opera*

"Now we can really sit back and do exactly the things we want to do."

—FREDDIE MERCURY, FEBRUARY 1976

(PREVIOUS) **Queen during the recording of *Jazz* in 1978. It would be the last time the band worked with their *A Night at the Opera* co-producer Roy Thomas Baker.**

(BELOW) **In the late 1970s, Queen began emphasizing their hard rock side; there would be no more "millionaire waltzes."**

QUEEN REMAINED on the album-tour-album-tour cycle for the next six years, easily navigating the constantly changing musical fashions and going from strength to strength.

When punk began agitating the UK music industry in the late 1970s, Queen seemed an easy target as a bloated, out-of-touch "dinosaur band." But they were able to slough off the criticism; Roger even said he liked the energy of these young upstarts. They also inadvertently gave a boost to the flagship punk band, the Sex Pistols. Queen had been scheduled to appear on the talk show *Today* on December 1, 1976, but had to cancel when Freddie needed to make an emergency visit to his dentist. In their place, EMI offered the Sex Pistols, who were also signed to the label. Goaded by the show's host, Bill Grundy, the band members spewed obscenities during their interview, shocking the viewers and resulting in alarmist headlines like THE FILTH AND THE FURY in the next day's *Daily Mirror*. Overnight, the Sex Pistols had become the best-known—and most notorious—music act in Britain.

Queen's own interactions with the group were less fraught. While recording *News of the World* at London's Wessex Studios in the summer of 1977, the band found the Sex Pistols working on *Never Mind the Bollocks* at the same venue. Pistols bassist Sid Vicious taunted Freddie about his pretentions of "bringing ballet to the masses," and Freddie responded in kind, calling him "Mr. Ferocious." But Brian and Roger recalled having pleasant conversations with guitarist Steve Jones and drummer Paul Cook.

Still, Queen could sense the changes in the wind and left behind their more dandyish proclivities. *News of the World*, released later in '77, emphasized the hard rock side of the band; it was time, in Brian's words, "to get back to basics and find some vitality again." There would be no more millionaire waltzes. Instead, the album served up the abrasive "Sheer Heart Attack" (previously written for the album of that name but still bursting with punk nihilism), the unbridled lust of "Get Down Make Love," and the one-two punch of the opening tracks "We Will Rock You" and "We Are the Champions." The latter two songs were also released on the same single, "Champions" being the A-side, each song tailor-made for audience participation and becoming perennial favorites at sporting events.

(RIGHT) **The celebratory "We Are the Champions" became an anthem at sporting events around the world.**

(OPPOSITE) **Brian on the road again, in 1978.**

(TOP) **Jazz marked the first time the band recorded at Mountain Studios in Montreaux, Switzerland; they liked the studio so much, they ended up buying it.**

(MIDDLE AND BOTTOM) **The 1978 Hungarian sleeve for "Bicycle Race" b/w "Fat Bottomed Girls."**

Roy Thomas Baker, fresh from producing the debut album by new wave band the Cars, returned to produce *Jazz* in 1978, with the band even purchasing one of the venues where they recorded the album, Mountain Studios in Montreux, Switzerland. *Jazz* featured some of the whimsy of the band's earlier years, with tongue-in-cheek numbers like "Bicycle Race" and "Fat Bottomed Girls," and the self-referential "Let Me Entertain You."

There was also Freddie's celebratory paean to sex and drugs, "Don't Stop Me Now," embodying a licentiousness that was also fully on display at the album's release party. Held at the Fairmont New Orleans hotel following their show in the city on October 31, 1978, the event was said to have cost $200,000 and was one of the most legendary nights of debauchery in rock history. "It was deliberately excessive," Brian later told *Mojo*. "Partly for our own enjoyment, partly for friends to enjoy, partly because it's exciting for record company people—and partly for the hell of it."

After the concert album *Live Killers* (1979), Queen hit their commercial peak in the US with the release of 1980's *The Game*, the first Queen album to use synthesizers. It was their only album to top the US charts and also featured their only stateside number one singles, "Crazy Little Thing Called Love" (a fun slice of rockabilly Freddie dreamed up while taking a bath) and John Deacon's funk infused "Another One Bites the Dust." Ironically, neither track had been earmarked for single release but had only been issued after DJs began playing the songs on the radio themselves. In the case of "Another One Bites the Dust," New York R&B station WBLS had been playing it, thinking it was by a Black act. It received a positive reception, and further encouragement came from Michael Jackson, who'd seen the band when they played the LA Forum in July 1980 and urged them to release it as a single. When it was finally issued, it became their biggest selling single up to that point and momentarily made them, as May recalled, "the biggest band in the world."

But then the band went into a holding pattern. In 1980, they recorded a suitably over-the-top soundtrack for Dino De Laurentiis' kitschy sci-fi fantasy *Flash Gordon*. In 1981, they enjoyed an international hit with "Under Pressure," a collaboration with David Bowie, released their first greatest hits collection (which would rack up sales of over 25 million copies), and played a highly successful string of dates in Argentina and Brazil (SOUTH AMERICA BITES THE DUST trumpeted one headline). But a subsequent tour of Central America later that year was more problematic, and a tour of Venezuela was cut short when the country's former president, Rómulo Betancourt, died, resulting in nationwide mourning. Mexican dates were plagued by uncooperative local crews, poor accommodations, constant demands for money from the authorities, and riotous crowds. After being pelted with batteries and rocks during their first performance in Puebla, Freddie angrily responded with a "*Adios, amigos*, you motherfuckers!" The band played only one more show before fleeing the country. The tour resulted in a substantial financial loss. As Brian later put it, "We escaped by the skin of our teeth."

And when the band went out on tour in support of 1982's *Hot Space* album, they were startled to find how far their stock had dropped in the US. There had already been some pushback over Freddie's changed appearance. By the end of the '70s, everyone in the band except Brian had cut their flowing locks. Freddie's leotards and Zandra Rhodes outfits were also consigned to the past in favor of leather jackets and trousers with matching leather cap. In the '80s, he began sporting the "Castro clone" look, named after San Francisco's predominantly gay Castro neighborhood where the fashion emerged: sneakers or boots, tight jeans, tight plaid shirts or T-shirts, short cropped hair, and a moustache.

When Freddie's moustache made its debut in the video for the 1980 single "Play the Game," fans responded by sending razors to Queen's office. There were also reports of razors being thrown onstage when the band performed. Freddie remained defiant. "Do you girls like this moustache?" he asked at one show. "Do you boys like the moustache? A lot of people hate it. I don't give a fuck, actually—it's my moustache, and I'm going to keep it!"

In stark contrast to The Game's success, Hot Space fared poorly in the US. The music plowed the same funk/dance rock territory as "Another One Bites the Dust," with a noticeable absence of guitar, reflecting Deacon's interest in funk and soul and what Mercury was hearing in the gay clubs he was frequenting. Even the song titles sounded like double entendres: "Body Language," "Back Chat," "Staying Power." America liked Queen as a rock band, not a disco act. Hot Space was not a record designed to appeal to a country that had drawn fifty thousand people to a "Disco Demolition Night" held at Comiskey Park in Chicago on July 12, 1979 (between a Chicago White Sox and Detroit Tigers double-header), to watch thousands of disco records get blown up. The event ended in a riot and the cancellation of the second game. As Brian conceded to Mark Blake, "I think Hot Space was a mistake. If only timing-wise. Disco was a dirty word by then."

While touring the US, the band saw for themselves how once sold-out venues now had empty seats. They made attempts to boost flagging ticket and record sales. Prior to their Madison Square Garden show on July 27, 1982, they took the unprecedented step of making an in-store appearance at a branch of the Crazy Eddie electronics store. Mercury, at least, seemed to regard it as a chore; one fan recalled him never speaking a

(ABOVE LEFT) **Brian and Roger in Toronto on August 30, 1980.**

(ABOVE RIGHT) **By 1979 Freddie had exchanged his flowing locks and leotards for short hair and tight trousers. But his moustache generated some controversy among his fans.**

Continued on page 141

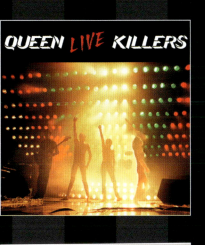

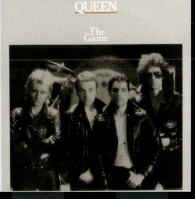

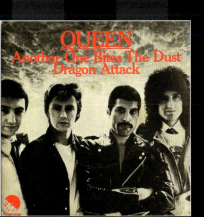

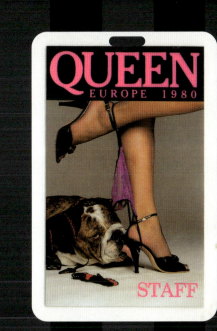

(LEFT TOP) **The cover of *Live Killers* showed Queen's impressive lighting rig.**

(LEFT CENTER) ***The Game* was the album where Queen hit their commercial peak in the US.**

(LEFT BOTTOM) **"Another One Bites the Dust" featured another John Deacon bassline destined to be sampled by innumerable other artists.**

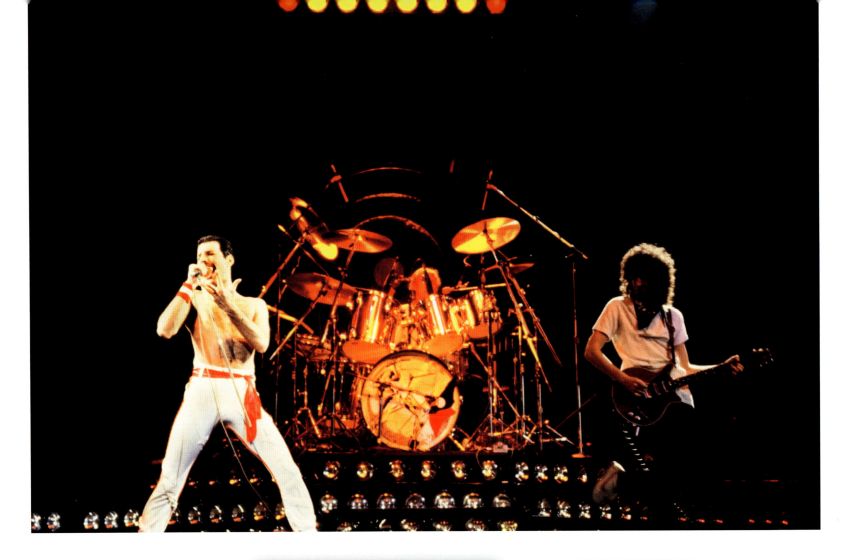

(TOP) **Queen during the US tour for** *Hot Space*. **The album hadn't fared well in America, and once sold-out venues now had empty seats.**

(RIGHT) **Brian later called** *Hot Space* **"a mistake. If only timing-wise. Disco was a dirty word by then."**

(OPPOSITE) **The** *Hot Space* **tour was the last time Freddie would perform live in the US.**

138 QUEEN AND A NIGHT AT THE OPERA

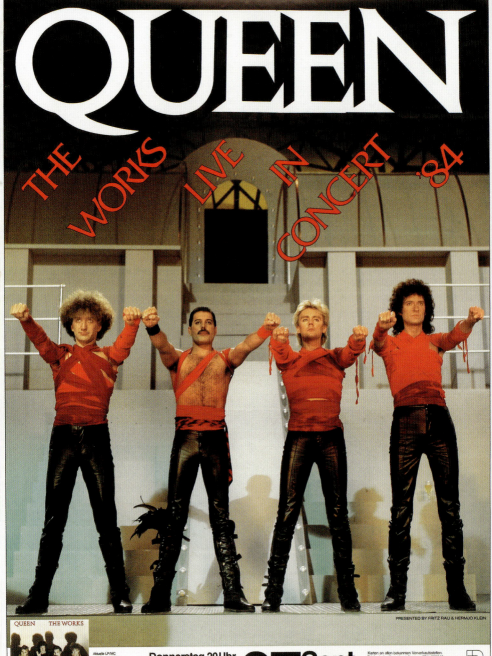

word as he signed the album covers placed in front of him. On September 25, they made their only live appearance on US television, performing "Crazy Little Thing Called Love" and "Under Pressure" on *Saturday Night Live*. But nothing helped. *Hot Space* peaked at #22 in the US. Where *The Game* had been a multiplatinum seller, *Hot Space* stalled at gold. Queen's September 15, 1982, concert at the Forum in LA turned out to be their last live US concert date.

Surprisingly, instead of trying to win the country back, Queen let America fall by the wayside, though select band members still visited the US on promotional trips. Perhaps they recognized America's disinterest had turned to active dislike in some quarters. MTV had banned the video for "Body Language" due to its racy content. And in 1984, the video for "I Want to Break Free," which featured the band members in drag, spoofing characters from the British soap opera *Coronation Street*, provoked widespread revulsion. Brian recalled television programmers "turning ashen" about the thought of broadcasting the video when he was on a US promo tour: "And they would say, 'No, we can't play this. We can't possibly play this. You know, it looks homosexual. . . .' I know that it really damaged our sort of whole relationship with certainly radio in this country and probably the public as well." As long as Queen played the macho rock card, Freddie's camp tendencies could be overlooked. But men in drag, even with tongue obviously in cheek, made things far too explicit for American tastes.

Queen took 1983 off, with all members but Deacon pursuing solo projects. By the time *The Works* was released in 1984, the band had jumped to Capitol Records in the US, unhappy with the promotion of *Hot Space*. The move didn't help—the album peaked at #23. In the UK, as always, the story was different, with the album reaching #2. But the band received fierce criticism in their native country and elsewhere when they played a series of shows at the Super Bowl in Sun City, Bophuthatswana, South Africa, in October, in violation of a United Nations anti-apartheid cultural boycott of the country. The band argued that they played before integrated audiences, and May pleaded their case before the Musicians Union in the UK. But they were still fined for breaking the union's rules.

Perhaps as a result of the criticism, Queen's tours in 1985 featured no UK dates. But then came Live Aid, on July 13, 1985, which offered a redemption. The sea of cheering people that greeted the band offered clear evidence that they were still much loved. And their set was acclaimed as the best performance of the day as soon as they left the stage. Queen was back and bigger than ever.

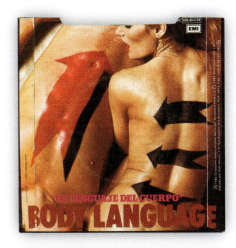

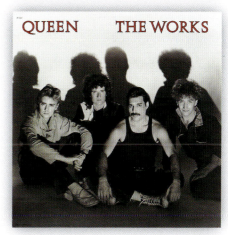

(ABOVE) ***The Works*** **continued Queen's commercial slide in the US, though it was a big hit in the UK and elsewhere. US sensibilities were also ruffled by the crossdressing in the video for "I Want to Break Free."**

QUEEN AFTER A NIGHT AT THE OPERA

THE MORALE BOOSTER: *Live Aid*

> "Live Aid was a shot in the arm."
>
> —ROGER TAYLOR, *MOJO*, 1999

Queen's shows were dazzling experiences known for their high production values: an elaborate lighting rig, explosions, dry ice. It's decidedly ironic that what's considered one of their greatest performances had none of those accoutrements and clocked in at a mere twenty minutes.

The Live Aid concerts, held on July 13, 1985, simultaneously at London's Wembley Stadium and Philadelphia's John F. Kennedy Stadium, were a continuation of the fundraising efforts for African famine relief that had begun with the release of the UK charity single "Do They Know It's Christmas?" in December 1984. The single was the brainchild of Boomtown Rats lead singer Bob Geldof, who brought together a supergroup of well-known performers to perform the song (which he'd cowritten with Midge Ure) under the joint name Band Aid. Once the single became a worldwide success, he began setting up charity concerts.

Queen had been disappointed they were not asked to participate on the single, Freddie publicly speculating it was because "I'm a bit old." But Geldof was quite interested in having them at Live Aid and contacted their manager, Jim Beach. After much discussion—Freddie had needed the most persuasion to participate—Queen signed on for the show.

The band prepared in a typically methodical fashion. Three days of rehearsals were held at London's Shaw Theatre, with clocks set up to ensure they didn't run over their allotted twenty-minute time slot. They focused on the hits: "Why bore them with something they've not heard before?" Roger later explained to *Mojo*. Freddie was also ill that week, and his doctor advised him to cancel. But there was no way he was going to miss this performance.

The London show opened with May and Taylor watching from the stadium's VIP box, Deacon preferring to wait backstage (when the group was later introduced to royal attendees Prince Charles and Princess Diana, Deacon, too nervous to meet the couple, sent a roadie in his place). Mercury was at home watching the show on TV with his new boyfriend, Jim Hutton, whom Mercury invited to accompany him to the event. They arrived at Wembley an hour before Queen's performance. Just before they took stage, Trip Khalaf, the band's sound tech, unobtrusively turned up the limiters on the main mixing board, meaning Queen would be louder than any other band.

At around quarter to 7 p.m., after Dire Straits' set, Freddie took a last swig of vodka, declared, "Let's do it," and Queen took the stage. They were attired in a very understated fashion, with Brian, John, and Roger wearing long trousers and long-sleeved white shirts, while Freddie wore light-blue jeans with a studded leather belt, a sleeveless white undershirt, white Adidas high-top tennis shoes, and a leather bracelet strapped around his right arm.

What followed was a breathtakingly well-paced performance. Freddie, at the piano, opened with Queen's signature song, "Bohemian Rhapsody," which, after the ballad section, segued into "Radio Ga Ga." Sawn-off mic stand now in hand, he dominated the stage as he strutted back and forth, a larger-than-life presence seeking to reach everyone, clear to the back of the stadium.

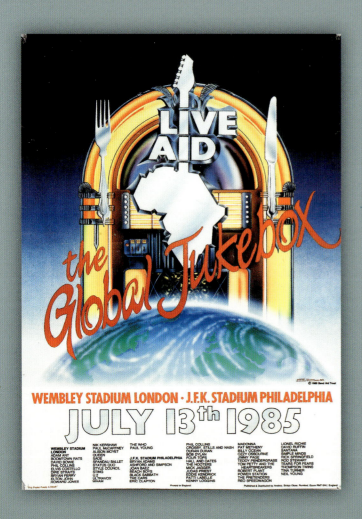

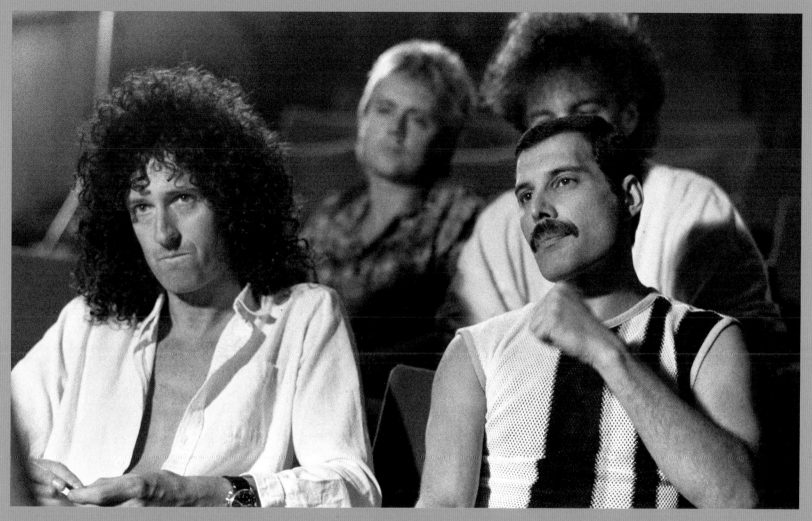

The band members take a break during rehearsals for their acclaimed Live Aid performance at London's Shaw Theatre. Their 20-minute set was packed with hit after hit.

At the end of "Hammer to Fall," he teasingly stood with his back to the audience, then bent over and looked back at the crowd between his legs. "This next song is only dedicated to beautiful people here tonight," he announced. "It means all of you. Thank you for coming along and making this a great occasion." Then it was into the buoyant "Crazy Little Thing Called Love."

And what better to conclude with than the stadium anthems "We Will Rock You" and "We Are the Champions"? As the crowd's upstretched arms waved back and forth while singing along, the band and audience were united in a euphoric moment. And then it was over, with the four band members taking a bow, and Freddie calling out, "Goodbye! We love you!"

Once backstage, he exclaimed, "Thank God that's over!" and had a large vodka. Such was the excitement Queen's set generated, it's often overlooked that Freddie and Brian made another appearance that day, performing a poignant rendition of "Is This the World We Created . . . ?" right before Paul McCartney's performance. The band members also appeared in the final sing-along of "Do They Know It's Christmas?" that closed Live Aid.

But it was the main set that made the greatest impression—to the band members themselves as much as their audience. "It wasn't just our fans we were playing to, it was *everyone's* fans," Brian said to journalist Lesley-Ann Jones. "Freddie really gave his all." And in the wake of the controversy surrounding the South African appearances, the positive attention was most welcome. "It was one day that I was proud to be involved in the music business," said John Deacon in one of his rare statements. "It was a good morale booster for us, too, because it showed us the strength of support we had in England, and it showed us what we had to offer as a band."

QUEEN AFTER A NIGHT AT THE OPERA

The next year was a victory lap, with *A Kind of Magic*, their fourth UK #1 album (#46 in the US) and a sold-out European/UK tour. The Top 10 UK hits "One Vision" and "A Kind of Magic" were anthems of optimism. "I got a sort of newfound force," said Freddie. "Suddenly, there was more left in Queen." He had designer Diana Moseley make an ermine cape, patterned after Napoleon's 1804 coronation robe, and a crown for him to wear during the tour; the ensemble made its debut at Queen's June 14 show in Paris. When a third night couldn't be added at Wembley Stadium, a final show was scheduled for Knebworth Park, outside Stevenage, Hertfordshire, on August 9. The concert drew an estimated 120,000 people. The twenty-four-song set spanned most of the band's career (there were no songs from the *Queen*, *Flash Gordon*, or *Jazz* albums), with some rock 'n' roll covers thrown in for fun. After "We Are the Champions," as their recording of "God Save the Queen" played while the band took their bows, Freddie strode to the front of the stage, wearing his cape and holding his crown aloft, and spoke his final words to the crowd: "Thank you, beautiful people! You've been a tremendous—you've been a really special audience. Thank you very much. Good night, sweet dreams, we love you."

Queen had just played their last show with Freddie Mercury.

DURING THAT FINAL show, Freddie seemed to indicate there was more to come from Queen, telling the audience at one point, "And earlier on there were rumors of us splitting up, but, I mean—fuck 'em. I mean really, look at this! How can you split up when you have an audience like this?" But offstage, it was another story. Just a few days prior, when the band was touring Spain, he'd told his bandmates, "I'm not going to be doing this forever. This is probably the last time." John Deacon had also shown a rare onstage fit of pique during the Knebworth concert, throwing his bass into the rack holding his other basses after the band had played "Radio Ga Ga." However, Freddie's decision wasn't based on a sudden flare-up of anger but something more serious.

It's never been clear exactly when Freddie knew he tested positive for HIV and then developed AIDS, or how and when he told those closest to him. The general consensus is that he knew by 1987, first telling the band's manager, Jim Beach, but forbidding him from telling anyone else, including the other members of Queen. Freddie eventually did tell his bandmates. "He only asked two things," Brian later recalled. "The first was, let's keep working. The other was when he was really sick, just come and visit me."

One reason Freddie wanted to keep the news private was that he was trying to avoid media scrutiny. He'd been dealt a terrible blow in 1987, when Paul Prenter, his former personal assistant (who'd begun working for Queen when he was employed by John Reid, during Reid's tenure as Queen's manager), sold his story to the British tabloid the *Sun*. The paper ran a series of articles featuring photographs provided by Prenter, with details about Freddie's supposed drug use and sex life, including naming former lovers who'd since died of AIDS and identifying Freddie's current boyfriend, Jim Hutton. For a man who never talked publicly about his private life, it must've been mortifying. "He couldn't believe anyone who had been so close to him could behave in so mean-spirited a way," Hutton later wrote in his memoir *Mercury and Me*. In the future, Freddie would let Brian and Roger handle press duties.

The title track of *A Kind of Magic* gave the band another Top 10 around the world, along with "One Vision," though the singles failed to crack the Top 40 in the US.

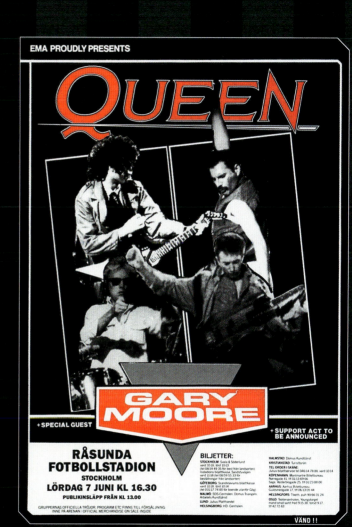

(LEFT AND OPPOSITE) **The *Live Magic* album chronicled Queen's last tour. These images were captured in Stockholm on June 7, 1986.**

(BELOW) ***Live Magic* was the first album released documenting what turned out to be Queen's last tour with Freddie Mercury. *The Miracle* was the first album where all the songs were jointly credited to the entire band.**

The *Live Magic* album (1986) chronicled Queen's last tour. Their next studio album, *The Miracle* (1989) topped the UK charts and five other countries (reaching #24 in the US). For the first time, all the songs were jointly credited to Queen rather than having individual songwriting credits, a decision which resolved a lot of inner-band conflict. All five of the album's singles reached the UK Top 30; in the US, only "I Want It All" made the US charts, peaking at #50 (and though sounding like one of Mercury's diva-esque demands, the song was written by May, whose second wife, Anita Dobson, was fond of the phrase).

On February 18, 1990, Freddie made his last appearance on stage with his bandmates when Queen received an award for Outstanding Contribution to Music at the annual BRIT Awards. After a short film introduction, the group came onstage to a standing ovation. Brian made most of the remarks; Roger managed to get in a quick "Thank you very much, it's been great!" followed by Freddie, looking gaunt and pale in a light blue suit, leaning into the mic to say, "Thank you, good night."

Before *The Miracle* was even released, the band were back in the studio working on their next album, *Innuendo*, with sessions continuing until November 1990. By now, the extent of Freddie's illness was apparent, but he pushed himself to keep working. Though Brian noticed how he faltered during the recording of the dramatic "The Show Must Go On," Queen's lead singer still managed to pull himself together to announce, "I'll fucking do it, darling," before recording the final vocal.

The month *Innuendo* was completed, Queen signed a deal with a new record company in the US, Hollywood Records, owned by the Walt Disney Company (now the

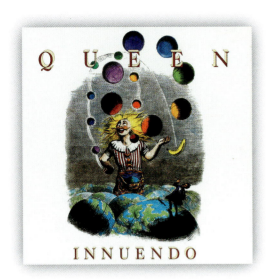

Innuendo topped the charts in five countries, including the UK. Though charting lower in the US, it was still certified gold.

Disney Music Group). Michael Eisner, then Disney's CEO, questioned the wisdom of signing the band, as they hadn't had a hit album in the US for a decade and refused to tour. But label head Peter Paterno pointed out the deal also included Queen's valuable back catalog, which alone made the $10 million price tag worthwhile. Nor was he worried about the rumors concerning Freddie's health, telling Eisner, "If he dies, as morbid as that sounds, that sells records too."

Innuendo was released in February 1991. There were the usual mixed reviews ("What is astounding is that in twenty years Queen have lost none of their appetite for music of the most grandiose banality," wrote the *Times*), but both the album and the title track topped the UK charts (the album reached #30 in the US; the single failed to chart). At the time of the album's release, Freddie was back at Mountain Studios, recording vocals for the tracks that would later appear on *Made in Heaven* and making videos for *Innuendo*'s singles. He recorded his final vocal, for the song "Mother Love," on May 22. His last video performance came on May 31, for "These Are the Days of Our Lives," a song by Taylor that's a bittersweet look back at the carefree days of one's youth. The video was made by Austrian director Rudi Dolezal, who'd first worked with the band on their "One Vision" video. It was shot in black and white to make the ravages of Freddie's illness less apparent, and Dolezal worked quickly, as Mercury was in obvious physical discomfort. But he nonetheless insisted on Dolezal filming one more take of him singing the song's final lines, after which he looked straight into the camera to whisper "I still love you."

"In these last few seconds of that song, he gives us a résumé of his whole life: 'I was a big superstar, but don't take it too seriously,'" Dolezal later told *People*. "And then, 'I still love you,' which is to the fans. Then he walks out of life. Even in his last moment, he planned his exit artistically. That's how he wanted it to be."

There were no more visits to the studio. Freddie now spent most of his time at his London home, Garden Lodge, which the press had staked out around the clock, though he did manage a final visit to Switzerland with Jim Hutton, staying in a flat he'd recently bought. Then, on November 23, Freddie released an official statement: "Following the enormous conjecture in the press over the last two weeks, I wish to confirm that I have been tested HIV positive and have AIDS. I felt it correct to keep this information private to date in order to protect the privacy of those around me. However, the time has now come for my friends and fans around the world to know the truth and I hope everyone will join with me, my doctors and all those worldwide in the fight against this terrible disease."

Queen's fans around the world barely had the time to digest this news before another announcement followed late on November 24 that Freddie had died that day of AIDS-related pneumonia. He was forty-five years old.

In keeping with Zoroastrian tradition, the funeral was held two days later at the West London Crematorium, the service conducted by two Parsi priests; a recording of Montserrat Caballé's version of "D'Amor Sull'Ali Rosee" ("On Love's Rose Colored Wings") from Verdi's *Il Trovatore* played as his coffin left the chapel. Back at Freddie's home, a growing pile of bouquets were left outside the door to Garden Lodge.

In the midst of grieving, business still had to be attended to. The release of Brian's solo single "Driven by You" was pushed back so as not to be seen as cashing in on the tragedy. But in December, "Bohemian Rhapsody"/"These Are the Days of Our Lives" was released in the UK as a benefit single, with proceeds earmarked for the AIDS charity the Terrence Higgins Trust. It entered the chart at #1.

Queen's post-Freddie era had begun.

Freddie announced that he had AIDS in a statement released on November 23, 1991. A day later came a second, sadder announcement that he had died at the age of 45.

8

Queen Is Dead, Long Live Queen!

"I often wonder, 'Is Freddie's spirit aware that we're still celebrating him and singing his music? Would Freddie like the way I sing?' And I hope, with all my heart, that he would approve of everything that we've been doing with these songs."

—ADAM LAMBERT,
NEW YORK POST, FEBRUARY 2023

(PREVIOUS) **The commemorative statue of Freddie, made by Irena Sedlecka, overlooks Lake Geneva in Montreux, Switzerland, where Freddie recorded his last songs.**

Made in Heaven **featured material dating back to 1980 and also included the last vocal Freddie recorded, for the song "Mother Love."**

AFTER FREDDIE'S DEATH, Queen released a statement: "We have lost the greatest and most beloved member of our family. We feel overwhelming grief that he has gone, sadness that he should be cut down at the height of his creativity, but above all great pride in the courageous way that he lived and died. It has been a privilege for us to have shared such magical times. As soon as we are able, we would like to celebrate his life in the style to which he was accustomed."

At the BRIT Awards on February 12, 1992, the remaining members of Queen accepted honors for "These Are the Days of Our Lives" as Best Single of 1991 and a posthumous honor for Freddie for Outstanding Contribution to British Music. They also announced the details of the celebration referred to in their statement: a benefit concert to be held on April 20, 1992. The organizing of the event would keep Brian, John, and Roger occupied for the next several months.

Freddie's death brought about a strong resurgence of interest in Queen's music. By December 1991, ten of the band's albums had reentered the UK Top 100. Following its release in the UK, "Bohemian Rhapsody" (backed with "The Show Must Go On") was reissued as a single in the US in February 1992, with proceeds donated to the Magic Johnson AIDS Foundation. It charted higher than on its original 1975 release, peaking at #2, further boosted by the song's inclusion in the film *Wayne's World*.

Queen's members felt that the tribute concert would be the band's last live hurrah. Now all that was left were the recordings that Freddie had managed to make before he died. But there was no agreement about what should be done with the material. So Brian and Roger spent the next few years working on their own music, with Brian releasing his first solo album, *Back to the Light*, in 1992. John kept a low profile; Freddie's death had hit him hard, and his public appearances would be increasingly infrequent. But he did join Roger onstage at a festival held at Cowdray Park, West Sussex, on September 18, 1993, playing a six-song set of Queen songs, with Roger on most vocals and Paul Young taking over on "Another One Bites the Dust."

Eventually, John and Roger began sifting through Queen's unreleased recordings to find tracks suitable for release, then overdubbing new bass and guitar parts. Brian still felt conflicted about the project but recalled that during his last year, Freddie had been clear about wanting the vocals he'd recorded to be released in some fashion. "Roger and John became very impatient with me and started working on the tapes," May later told *Q*. "I didn't want this stuff to go out without my involvement, so I took the tapes off them, felt that they'd done it wrong, and spent months putting it all back together." He described compiling the album as "like assembling a jigsaw puzzle," adding, "I wouldn't have put my seal of approval on it if I hadn't thought it was up to standard."

The final product, *Made in Heaven*, was released on November 6, 1995, and drew on material going as far back as sessions for *The Game* ("It's a Beautiful Day"). Previously recorded vocals from *The Works* and Freddie's solo releases were given new musical backings; three songs ("Mother Love," "You Don't Fool Me," and "A Winter's Tale") were from Freddie's final sessions. Reviews were largely positive ("A more than worthy epitaph to the great entertainer," wrote the *Sunday Times*, and the album topped the charts in the UK and eleven other countries but limped to #58 in the US. The cover featured Irena Sedlecká's bronze statue of Freddie, based on the image used on the 1992 tribute concert poster, his right arm held aloft in triumph. The statue was later installed in Montreux, overlooking Lake Geneva.

NIGHT TO REMEMBER:
The Freddie Mercury Tribute Concert

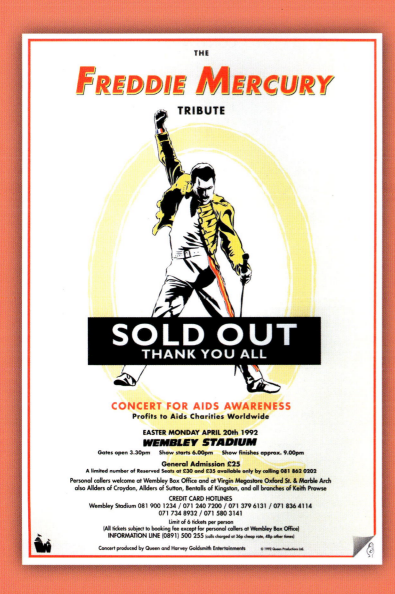

Tickets for The Freddie Mercury Tribute: Concert for AIDS Awareness went on sale on February 13, 1992, the day after the show had first been announced at the BRIT Awards. They sold out in three hours, before the names of any participants had been announced. It was an act of faith that greatly touched Queen's remaining members, not least because the show was also planned as a charity event.

With the concert set for Easter Monday, April 20, 1992, there was little time to waste. Rehearsals began on March 27 in London, later moving to Bray Studios in Berkshire (best known as the location where Hammer Film Productions shot their horror movies). In a sign of things to come, John Deacon was initially hesitant about participating, meaning early rehearsals had Whitesnake bassist Neil Murray in his place. Deacon eventually changed his mind and decided to appear.

Wembley Stadium was the obvious location, as it was the site of Queen's triumph at Live Aid in 1985. Crews began assembling the massive stage on April 15; crowds began lining up for entry the day before the show, on April 19. The gates finally opened at 4 p.m. the following day

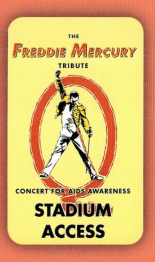

QUEEN IS DEAD, LONG LIVE QUEEN!

Queen's remaining members welcomed the audience at the Freddie Mercury Tribute concert for what Brian called "the biggest sendoff in history!" "You can cry all you like," Roger told the crowd.

Brian, Roger, and John received a thunderous ovation when they first took the stage to make some preconcert remarks, Brian calling the event "the biggest sendoff in history!" for their bandmate. "Tell the world AIDS affects us all," Roger said, adding, "You can cry all you like." It was left to John to introduce the first act, Metallica. The concert's first half also featured Guns N' Roses, U2 beamed in by satellite, and Spinal Tap providing comic relief. Extreme got a huge reception by being the first act to play any Queen songs; a similar response came when May joined Def Leppard for a run through "Now I'm Here." Elizabeth Taylor made what was probably the show's most unexpected appearance, deftly swatting away hecklers as she urged the crowd, "Protect yourselves! Every time you have sex, use a condom!"

The concert's second half featured the real highlights, as May, Taylor, and Deacon backed a rotating series of lead vocalists who tackled various Queen songs. Joe Elliott (Def Leppard) and Slash (Guns N' Roses) got the party started with "Tie Your Mother Down," followed by a who's who of rock stars. Roger Daltrey took on "I Want It All." Robert Plant stumbled through "Innuendo" but redeemed himself on "Crazy Little Thing Called Love." Top marks went to George Michael's impassioned performance of "Somebody to Love," also featuring the London Community Gospel Choir. Lisa Stansfield not only performed "I Want to Break Free" but also referenced the song's video, coming onstage pushing a vacuum cleaner, as Freddie had done in the promo clip. David Bowie shared vocals on "Under Pressure" with Annie Lennox,

"Freddie would have said, 'Darling, Wembley Stadium? Are you sure it's big enough?'"

—ROGER TAYLOR, *MOJO*, 2005

invited Ian Hunter to the stage for "All the Young Dudes," performed his own "Heroes," then movingly went down on one knee to recite the Lord's Prayer.

May and longtime Queen keyboardist Spike Edney delivered a sensitive performance of a new song, "Too Much Love Will Kill You." Axl Rose shared "Bohemian Rhapsody" with Elton John. There had been controversy about Rose's participation due to the perceived homophobia in GNR's "One in a Million." Elton defended the choice but was more put out when Rose failed to turn up for any rehearsals; after being denied admission to Rose's dressing room because "Axl's sleeping," he ranted to the members of Def Leppard, "What the fuck's wrong with that guy?" But their performance came off without a hitch, Rose later returning for "We Will Rock You."

At first, Liza Minnelli seemed an odd choice to end the show with "We Are the Champions," but it actually made perfect sense. Who better to add a touch of theatrical glamour than the star of *Cabaret*, the film that Freddie had adored? Certainly, the crowds joining in to sing along seemed to agree. As the other performers and musicians returned to the stage to join in, the concert climaxed as it was always meant to, in a moment of joyous celebration. It was a cathartic, emotional experience for the fans who had wanted—needed—to pay tribute to Freddie Mercury's remarkable life.

A crowd of seventy-two thousand people had filled the stadium; hundreds of thousands more listened or watched the show on radio and television. Proceeds from the concert (estimates ranging wildly, from $8 million to $35 million) were used to establish the AIDS charity the Mercury Phoenix Trust. An edited version of the concert was released on VHS in 1993 and later on DVD and Blu-ray. And the Mercury Phoenix Trust continues its work today.

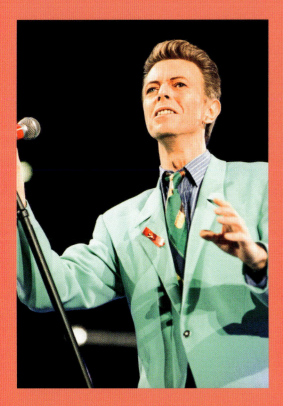

David Bowie's set featured an impromptu recitation of the Lord's Prayer. Elton John and Guns N' Roses lead singer Axl Rose shared vocals on "Bohemian Rhapsody." Metallica, featuring James Hetfield, opened the show with a three-song set.

QUEEN IS DEAD, LONG LIVE QUEEN!

John Deacon's last public appearance with May and Taylor came on January 17, 1997, when they performed at the premiere of Maurice Béjart's *A Ballet for Life*, at the Théâtre de Chaillot in Paris. The ballet was a tribute to both Mercury and Argentinian dancer Jorge Donn (who had also died of AIDS) and featured music by Queen and Mozart. The three members of Queen, along with Spike Edney on keyboards, backed Elton John during "The Show Must Go On." That October, May, Taylor, and Deacon came together one last time to record the final Queen song, "No-One But You (Only the Good Die Young)," written by May, he and Taylor sharing the lead vocal. It was released in November 1997 on the compilation *Queen Rocks* and as a single, reaching #13 in the UK (it failed to chart in the US).

And then Deacon effectively retired from public life. "John just decided he couldn't handle people," Roger told Mark Blake. "Not just Queen, he didn't want to be around people. He was quiet even in Queen and not as mentally rugged as we were." So it would be left to Brian and Roger to carry Queen's legacy into the new millennium.

ON MARCH 19, 2001, Queen was inducted into the Rock and Roll Hall of Fame, the ceremony held at the Waldorf-Astoria Hotel in New York. The band was inducted by Dave Grohl and Taylor Hawkins of Foo Fighters, both longtime fans (the band regularly covered Queen's songs in concert). "As a live band, Queen kinda kicked everybody's ass," Hawkins said. "Queen were my first concert, and every concert since has been a bit of a letdown."

Brian and Roger accepted the awards (Deacon was a no-show). In their own comments, Roger joked that the induction "means more than all the Grammys we never got," while Brian sent out thanks "to the people of America for taking us to your hearts over the last thirty years," adding, "We're a little sad that Freddie and John can't be with us but they both send their love." As a special surprise, Roger then invited Freddie's mother Jer to the stage to accept her son's award; she received a standing ovation as she made her way through the audience. Brian and Roger then traded vocals on a performance of "We Will Rock You," next inviting Grohl and Hawkins back to the stage for a rousing "Tie Your Mother Down."

The two also wanted to find ways to breathe new life into Queen's impressive catalog, and the following year, the jukebox musical *We Will Rock You* brought Queen's music back to the stage in a show that became an international hit. Ideas about a Queen musical had been discussed since the mid-1990s, initially with a more biographical slant. In the end, Ben Elton, who'd previously been a scriptwriter for the UK sitcoms *The Young Ones* and *Blackadder*, came up with a fictional storyline, set in a dystopian future where rock music is banned. "The story is slightly crass," Roger admitted to the *Telegraph*. "But I think it has its good points."

We Will Rock You opened on May 14, 2002, at London's Dominion Theatre, with a replica of Irena Sedlecká's statue of Freddie towering above the entrance on the theater's marquee. Reviews were predictably harsh. The *Guardian* called it "both pretentious and insultingly simple-minded"; the *Daily Mail* simply wrote it off as "shallow, stupid and totally vacuous." But audience support was strong, as always. Fittingly, the show later won the Audience Award for Most Popular Show at the 2011 Laurence Olivier Awards (the UK equivalent of the Tonys). There have since been several successful productions around the world, including a year-long run at the Paris Las Vegas casino.

May and Taylor made occasional guest appearances during the show's UK run (and at select performances in other countries) during the encore closing number, "Bohemian

Dave Grohl joined Brian and Roger on stage when Queen was inducted into the Rock and Roll Hall of Fame in 2001.

QUEEN IS DEAD, LONG LIVE QUEEN!

THE NEW LEAD SINGERS:
Rodgers + Lambert Join the Fold

Queen have toured with two lead singers since Freddie's death, one they'd first seen during their pre-Queen days, the other a rising star from reality TV.

Paul Bernard Rodgers was born in Middlesbrough, England, on December 17, 1949. He first played bass in a local band called the Roadrunners, later becoming lead vocalist. On moving to London, he joined the band Free in 1968, a blues-rock band whose biggest hit was "All Right Now" (cowritten by Rodgers). Freddie saw Free when they played a show at Ealing Technical College; Brian and Roger also encountered the band when Smile shared the bill with Free at a benefit concert at London's Royal Albert Hall on February 27, 1969.

After Free split up, Rodgers formed Bad Company, who found success with hits like "Can't Get Enough" and "Feel Like Makin' Love." He subsequently joined The Firm with Jimmy Page, headed up his own group, the Paul Rodgers Band, and also turned up for various Bad Company reunions.

When he crossed paths with Brian May at the Fender Stratocaster anniversary concert on September 24, 2004, his future wife, Cynthia Kereluk, immediately noted the chemistry between the two musicians. "All you need is a drummer," she told them, prompting Brian to respond, "Well, I do know a drummer . . . ." Roger jumped at the chance of bringing Queen back to life again. "It's been in the back of our minds to do something like this for a long time," he told *Mojo*, "but Brian and I couldn't think of how to do it properly, so it kept being put on the back burner."

The Rodgers-May-Taylor lineup (with additional musicians on bass, guitar, and keyboards) made its debut on November 11, 2004, when Queen was inducted into the UK Music Hall of Fame. Pleased by the results, "Queen + Paul Rodgers" went out on tour the following year (John Deacon declined to be involved, preferring to stay in retirement). Sets mixed together Queen and Rodgers' songs, with subsequent tours in 2006 and 2008. The latter year also saw the release of an album of original music, *The Cosmos Rocks*, a solid hard rock record that generated the usual mixed reviews (*Billboard*: "It's a shame that the end result, the first under the Queen name in 13 years, is not very memorable"), and, more tellingly, minimal sales (reaching #5 in the UK, where it was certified silver, for sales of sixty thousand copies, and #47 in the US). The band also released two live albums and a live DVD.

In 2009, Rodgers chose to rejoin Bad Company for a summer tour, and the Queen + Paul Rodgers collaboration amicably came to an end. But it wasn't long before a connection was made for the next stage of Queen's touring life.

> **"Paul's range is phenomenal."**
> —ROGER TAYLOR ON PAUL RODGERS

On May 20, 2009, Brian and Roger made a surprise appearance on the reality show *American Idol*, playing "We Are the Champions" behind the top two contestants for Season 8: Kris Allen and Adam Lambert. Allen was chosen as the winner, but May and Taylor kept their eyes on Lambert, sensing his potential.

Adam Mitchel Lambert was born in Indianapolis, Indiana, on January 29, 1982, after which the family moved to San Diego, California. He began performing in local theater productions as a child and moved to Los Angeles to pursue an entertainment career after graduating from high school in 2000. His first job was working on a cruise ship; he then found work in musical theater, appearing in a touring production of *Wicked* and a European tour of *Hair*, among other gigs. He also worked as a session musician.

He auditioned for *American Idol* with Michael Jackson's "Rock with You" and Queen's "Bohemian Rhapsody." While on *Idol*, photos of him kissing another man appeared online; some felt the resulting controversy led to his only getting a second-place win on the show. Following *Idol*, he pursued a solo career, releasing the album *For Your Entertainment* in 2009 and touring the following year.

In 2011, Brian and Roger tapped him to join Queen. Their first performance was a short set at the MTV EMA Awards in Belfast on June 11, 2011. The "Queen + Adam Lambert" tours began the following year and have continued to this day. Lambert has proved to be a more comfortable fit for Queen than Paul Rodgers, who admitted he had trouble with the band's more "theatrical" numbers, as he put it. Brian described Adam to *Uncut* as "a gift from God—I cannot believe we have been delivered someone so unbelievably talented." For his part, Adam's been happy to keep the Queen fires burning, telling the *New York Post*, "I feel, in many ways, that I'm of service to Brian and Roger so that they can get onstage and perform their songs. And you couldn't ask for a better job."

"**Adam is the first person we've encountered who can do all the Queen catalogue without blinking.**"

—BRIAN MAY ON ADAM LAMBERT

(OPPOSITE) **Eighteen years after the 1986 tour, Queen was back, with Paul Rodgers stepping into Freddie Mercury's shoes.**

(ABOVE RIGHT) **Adam Lambert has been Queen's lead singer since 2011; Brian called him "a gift from God."**

QUEEN IS DEAD, LONG LIVE QUEEN!

Rhapsody," and occasionally during other songs as well. But they each yearned to do more than simply make guest appearances. Given the strength of George Michael's appearance at the Freddie tribute concert, it was suggested that he join Queen as lead vocalist, and over the years, other names were put forward. The most serious contender, according to May, was Robbie Williams, who recorded a version of "We Will Rock You" with May and Taylor for the 2001 film *A Knight's Tale*. Deacon was asked to participate but declined. He was later quoted as saying, "I've heard what they did and it's rubbish. It is one of the greatest songs ever written but I think they ruined it." Though Deacon was no longer an active member of Queen, he was still involved in the group's business decisions. Perhaps his public denouncing of the song stopped in its tracks the idea of using Williams on a more permanent basis.

Everything changed on the night of September 24, 2004, when Brian performed at a concert celebrating the fiftieth anniversary of the Fender Stratocaster guitar, held at Wembley Arena (a smaller venue adjacent to Wembley Stadium). Brian ended up performing Free's "All Right Now" with the band's lead singer, Paul Rodgers. He had such a good time that he approached Roger about reviving Queen with Paul in Freddie's place. Things moved quickly. Two months later, Queen + Paul Rodgers debuted at the UK Music Hall of Fame's induction ceremony on November 11, 2004, and the following year, the newly revived Queen went out on tour.

Queen + Paul Rodgers stayed together through 2008. They even released a new album, *The Cosmos Rocks*, which reached #5 in the UK and #47 in the US (though it reached the Top 20 in *Billboard*'s Top Rock Albums chart). As May conceded, "It seems that, on record at least, most Queen fans just want to hear the original line-up." There was also a feeling the lineup had run its course, and after a final date in Rio de Janeiro in November 2008, it was announced that the group were disbanding.

But there was no shortage of opportunities for May and Taylor to continue playing Queen songs. Indeed, it was just such an opportunity that led them to find their next lead singer, when they backed Adam Lambert on May 20, 2009, during the finals for *American Idol*. Two years later, they performed together at the MTV EMA Awards in Belfast on November 6, 2011, and the following year, Queen + Adam Lambert went out on their first tour. As of this writing, the lineup is still going strong.

IN ADDITION TO keeping Queen's legacy alive through performance, Brian and Roger were now heavily involved in promoting the Queen brand in other ways. There was a steady stream of compilations and reissues. *Queen Forever*, released in 2014, featured some previously unreleased material: "Let Me in Your Heart Again," recorded during sessions for *The Works*; a ballad version of "Love Kills" (a more synth-driven version had appeared on the 1984 *Metropolis* soundtrack); and "There Must Be More to Life Than This." The latter song had originally been recorded by Mercury as a duet with Michael Jackson. It was then recorded with Queen during *Hot Space* sessions but hadn't made the final track listing; it was finally recorded for Mercury's *Mr. Bad Guy* album. The *Queen Forever* version featured the *Hot Space* backing track and Mercury's and Jackson's vocals.

The band's songs were also increasingly featured in films, television shows, and video games, with "We Will Rock You," "We Are the Champions," and "Under Pressure" proving to be the most popular. More controversially, the band's music was also appearing in numerous commercials. Using "I'm in Love with My Car" in an ad for Jaguars does make sense. But elsewhere, "Love of My Life" was featured in an ad where a man sings it to his favorite beverage, Carlsberg beer. An ad parodying the "Bohemian Rhapsody" video sang the praises of Mountain Dew. "I Want It All" has been used in ads hawking everything from credit cards to home insurance to Twix candy bars. It was a dismaying development for many rock fans, who disliked seeing songs they had an emotional attachment to reduced to jingles. But Taylor, for one, was unrepentant, telling a journalist, "I don't want Queen's music to just be on some piece of vinyl from the 1970s. I want our music to be on the radio and to be everywhere."

And though the band were still touring, Roger helped launch an official Queen tribute band, Queen Extravaganza, in 2012. But the most important Queen-related release of the twenty-first century to date, one that boosted Queen's profile immeasurably, was one that had been in development for a decade: the biopic *Bohemian Rhapsody*.

(OPPOSITE) **The musical *We Will Rock You* received critical brickbat but enjoyed great success with audiences. Scriptwriter Ben Elton, at left, joins Roger and Brian at a rehearsal in Sydney, Australia, on October 8, 2004.**

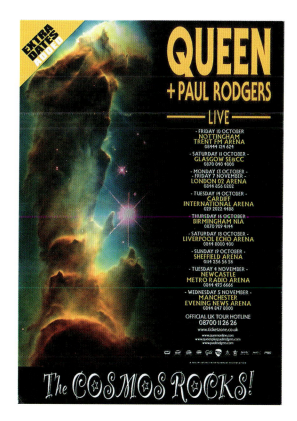

QUEEN IS DEAD, LONG LIVE QUEEN!

Rami Malek won an Oscar for his performance as Freddie in the film *Bohemian Rhapsody*; Gwilym Lee played Brian.

Discussions about a film had begun in 2008. It was announced publicly in 2010, with British comedian Sacha Baron Cohen the front-runner to play Freddie. Though Brian called the potential casting of Cohen "perfect," he nonetheless sounded cautious about the prospect of doing a movie, telling the *Daily Record*, "Freddie's legacy is very precious and we have a great responsibility not to mess it up."

But three years later, Cohen had left the project, citing "creative differences." He later told radio host Howard Stern he'd wanted to do more of a "warts and all" story, whereas Queen preferred to do something more family-friendly. Brian denied Cohen's account, telling the *Daily Mail*, "Are we the kind of people who have ever ducked from the truth? I don't think so."

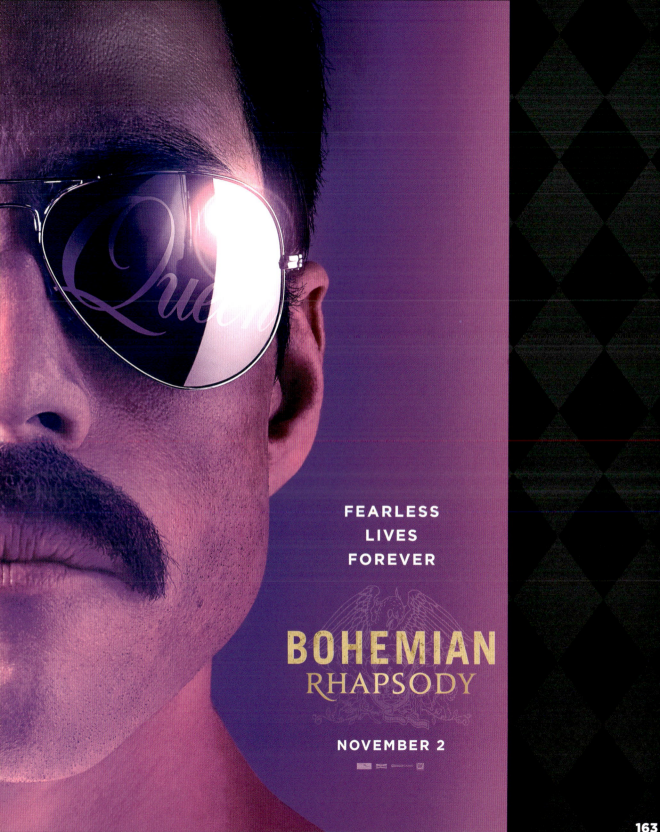

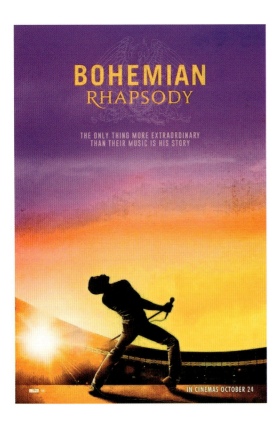

Whatever the reasons, a new Freddie had to be found. British actor Ben Whishaw was the next hopeful, but negotiations stalled; various directors also came and went. Finally, Rami Malek was cast in 2016, with Bryan Singer signed to direct. As filming was nearing its end, Singer was fired in December 2017, ostensibly because he hadn't returned to the set since Thanksgiving break, though there were rumors of tensions between Singer and the cast and crew. Dexter Fletcher replaced Singer as director, though Singer retained his director's credit.

Bohemian Rhapsody finally had its world premiere at Wembley Arena on October 23, 2018. It quickly set records as the highest-grossing musical biopic of all time, grossing over $900 million worldwide. The film's soundtrack reached #3 in the UK; in the US, it reached #2 in *Billboard*'s main chart and topped the magazine's Top Rock Albums and Top Soundtrack Albums charts. Malek's star turn as Freddie earned him the Oscar for Best Actor, the film also winning Oscars for Best Film Editing, Sound Editing, and Sound Mixing.

But there was controversy too. In a story with so much real drama, it's mystifying that it was felt necessary to invent details for "dramatic effect." In real life, no one was upset that Mercury wanted to make solo albums (indeed, by that point, Taylor and May had already released their own solo records). Nor did he inform his bandmates that he had AIDS while they rehearsed for their Live Aid appearance. Due to time constraints, a biopic is by necessity a compressed version of the complete story. But these were events that hadn't even happened.

And while the film didn't shy away from depicting Freddie's gay life—though ostensibly about Queen, the film is really Freddie Mercury's story—critics took issue with how that life was generally presented in a negative light. Mercury's assistant Paul Prenter is cast as the gay predator who leads him astray (as well as not passing on the invitation to perform at Live Aid, which didn't happen in real life). Instead of showing all the band members enjoying typical rock 'n' roll partying, May, Deacon, and Taylor are seen hastily leaving a party emulating the *Jazz* release-party bacchanal, murmuring "This isn't our scene" like prim maiden aunts. Throughout the film, the choices Mercury makes in his personal life are shown as being problematic, especially in contrast to the safe, settled lives of his bandmates and ex-girlfriend.

The film was an opportunity to examine Freddie's complexities and contradictions. Here was a man coming to terms with his sexuality at a time when such matters weren't spoken about openly, who nonetheless named his band Queen, wore a T-shirt in the "Don't Stop Me Now" video promoting New York gay sex club The Mineshaft, and teased critics by saying, "I'm gay as a daffodil, dear!" The split between his private and public life was further exacerbated by the band's fame and the pressures of maintaining commercial success. But the film chooses to play it safe, even providing redemption where none existed, as in the scene showing Freddie stopping by his parents' home while on the way to Live Aid to introduce them to his boyfriend Jim Hutton—a heartwarming moment that never happened.

"The film's reluctance to deal with Mercury's sexuality is catastrophic because his sexuality is so connected to the art of Queen that the two cannot be separated out," critic Sheila O'Malley wrote. Similarly, Aja Romano wrote in *Vox* that *Bohemian Rhapsody* "strips Mercury of a part of his identity that was as vital to his success as his four-octave vocal range." But a film that addressed such issues would likely not have received the desired PG-13 rating or have become such a box office success. As *IndieWire* put it, "the legend is always prioritized over the truth, even when the truth was surely far more interesting." Successful as it was, *Bohemian Rhapsody* was also something of a lost opportunity.

"IT WAS PROBABLY the most important album we ever made," Roger said of *A Night at the Opera*. Nothing was ever the same for Queen after its release. Its success enabled them to make that leap into the pantheon of eternal rock superstars. It became the cornerstone on which their legend was ultimately built. But the songs are not mere nostalgia. They come alive again in performance, when the audience sings along to "Love of My Life"; when Roger gets his moment in the spotlight in "I'm in Love with My Car"; when the main set closes, naturally, with "Bohemian Rhapsody." These are songs that have forged an unbreakable bond between band and audience; these are songs that the audience feels are much theirs as the band's.

And that was Queen's essential magic. Beneath all the theatricality, the flash and extravagance, the pomp and circumstance, this was a band that wanted nothing more than to make sure the audience was included in their fun—that you were as much a part of the show as the costumes, the lights, the pyrotechnics. Queen always strove to establish a connection with their audience, and the fans responded in kind, with a steadfast loyalty (*Guinness World Records* sites the Official Queen Fan Club as "the longest running fan club for a band"). For despite what the critics have said, Queen were never elitist. They wanted to welcome everybody to their Night at the Opera.

> **"It was probably the most important album we ever made."**
>
> —ROGER TAYLOR

A Night at the Opera Tour Dates

14–15.11.1975	Empire Theatre	Liverpool, GBR
16.11.1975	Coventry Theatre	Coventry, GBR
17–18.11.1975	Colston Hall	Bristol, GBR
19.11.1975	Capitol Theatre	Cardiff, GBR
21.11.1975	Odeon	Taunton, GBR
23.11.1975	Winter Gardens	Bournemouth, GBR
24.11.1975	Gaumont	Southampton, GBR
26.11.1975	Free Trade Hall	Manchester, GBR (two shows)
29–30.11.1975	Hammersmith Odeon	London, GBR
01–03.12.1975	Hammersmith Odeon	London, GBR
07.12.1975	Civic Hall	Wolverhampton, GBR
08.12.1975	Guildhall	Preston, GBR
09–10.12.1975	Odeon	Birmingham, GBR
11.12.1975	City Hall	Newcastle, GBR
13.12.1975	Caird Hall	Dundee, GBR
14.12.1975	Capitol	Aberdeen, GBR
15–16.12.1975	The Apollo	Glasgow, GBR
24.12.1975	Hammersmith Odeon	London, GBR
27.01.1976	Palace Theater	Waterbury, CT
29–30.01.1976	Music Hall	Boston, MA
31.01.1976	Tower Theatre	Philadelphia, PA
01–02.02.1976	Tower Theatre	Philadelphia, PA
05–08.02.1976	Beacon Theatre	New York, NY
11–12.02.1976	Masonic Auditorium	Detroit, MI
13.02.1976	Riverfront Coliseum	Cincinnati, OH
14.02.1976	Public Hall	Cleveland, OH
15.02.1976	Toledo Sports Arena	Toledo, OH
18.02.1976	Saginaw Civic Center	Saginaw, MI
19.02.1976	Veterans Memorial Auditorium	Columbus, OH
20.02.1976	New Stanley Theater	Pittsburgh, PA
22–24.02.1976	Auditorium Theatre	Chicago, IL
26.02.1976	Kiel Auditorium	St. Louis, MO
27.02.1976	Indianapolis Convention Center	Indianapolis, IN
28.02.1976	Dane County Coliseum	Madison, WI
29.02.1976	Allen County War Memorial Coliseum	Fort Wayne, IN
02.03.1976	Milwaukee Auditorium	Milwaukee, WI
03.03.1976	St. Paul Civic Center Auditorium	St. Paul, MN
07.03.1976	Berkeley Community Theatre	Berkeley, CA
09.03.1976	Santa Monica Civic Auditorium (two shows)	Santa Monica, CA
10–11.03.1976	Santa Monica Civic Auditorium	Santa Monica, CA
12.03.1976	San Diego Sports Arena	San Diego, CA
22.03.1976	Nippon Budokan	Tokyo, JPN
23.03.1976	Aichi Taikukan	Nagoya, JPN
24.03.1976	Kosei Kaikan	Himeji, JPN
26.03.1976	Kyuden Kinen Taikukan	Fukuoka, JPN
11.04.1976	Entertainments Centre	Perth, AUS
14–15.04.1976	Apollo Stadium	Adelaide, AUS
17–18.04.1976	Horden Pavilion	Sydney, AUS
19–20.04.1976	Festival Hall	Melbourne, AUS
22.04.1976	Festival Hall	Brisbane, AU
01–02.09.1976	Playhouse Theatre	Edinburgh, GBR
10.09.1976	Cardiff Castle	Cardiff, GBR
18.09.1976	Hyde Park	London, GBR

Bibliography

ARTICLES

Arnold, Chuck. "Adam Lambert on Queen Gig: "Would Freddie Mercury Like the Way I Sing?" *New York Post*, February 24, 2023.

Barnes, Ken. Review of *Queen II*. *Rolling Stone*, June 20, 1974.

Benedict, David. "Very, Very Frightening." *The Guardian*, May 18, 2002.

Benton, Michael. "Standing Up for the Queen." *Melody Maker*, July 28, 1973.

Booth, Samantha. "Sacha Baron Cohen Is Perfect to Play Freddie Mercury but We Can't Mess Up His Legacy, Says Brian May." *Daily Record*, April 27, 2011.

Cavanagh, David. "Freddie Felt His Talent Was Building Other People's Swimming Pools." *Uncut*, October 2008.

Clark, Rick. "Roy Thomas Baker: Taking Chances and Making Hits." *Mix*, April 1, 1999.

Cohen, Mitchell. "Queen: The New British Invasion." *Phonograph Record*, March 1976.

Coon, Caroline. "Queen Bee." *Melody Maker*, December 21, 1974.

Cummings, Howard. "The Outspoken, Irreverent Roy Thomas Baker." *R-e/p*, 1979.

Cunningham, Mark. "Roy Thomas Baker and Gary Langan: The Making of Queen's 'Bohemian Rhapsody.'" *Sound on Sound*, October 1995.

Deevoy, Adrian. "'It's Obvious That It Wasn't Going to Work . . . It Wouldn't Suspend Your Disbelief': Brian May on Sacha Baron Cohen's Claims over Freddie Mercury Biopic." *The Daily Mail*, April 9, 2016.

Doherty, Harry. "Queen: Brian May—The Power behind Queen's Throne." *Melody Maker*, December 6, 1975.

Doherty, Harry. "Queen's Evidence." *Melody Maker*, November 22, 1975.

Doherty, Harry. "We Do the Best We Can." *Melody Maker*, September 18, 1976.

Duncan, Robert. "Audio: Queen's Freddie Mercury (1976)," rocksbackpages.com

Dry, Jude. "'Bohemian Rhapsody' Doesn't Straightwash, but It's Confused about Freddie Mercury's Sexuality." *IndieWire*, November 2, 2018.

Erskine, Pete. Review of "Bohemian Rhapsody." *New Musical Express*, November 1, 1975.

Fletcher, Gordon. Review of *Queen*. *Rolling Stone*, December 6, 1973.

Girardet, Edward. "Rural Rock: Queen, Oasis and the Ridge Farm Story." *Global Geneva*, April 21, 2020.

Greene, Andy. "Q&A: Queen, Adam Lambert Talk New Tour, Pressure and John Deacon." *Rolling Stone*, March 6, 2014.

Gross, Terry. "Fresh Air's Summer Music Interviews: Queen Guitarist Brian May." NPR, August 29, 2022.

Hann, Michael. "Brian May: 'I Never Have a Single Day without Thinking about Freddie.'" *The Guardian*, August 5, 2021.

Hotten, Jon. "'I've Lived, I Really Have. I've Done It All. I Love the Fact That I Make People Happy': The Life and Times of Rock's Most Outrageous Star, Freddie Mercury." *Classic Rock*, November 24, 2023.

Hunt, Elle. "Brian May: 'Nothing Could Ever Top Playing on the Roof of Buckingham Palace with No Safety Net.'" *The Guardian*, July 13, 2023.

Huntman, Ruth. "Brian May: Me, My Dad and 'the Old Lady.'" *The Guardian*, October 18, 2014.

Ingham, Jonh. "Mercury Rising: The Queen Interview." *Sounds*, January 31, 1976.

Ingham, Jonh. "Queen: A Riot at the Opera." *Sounds*, November 29, 1975.

Jones, Allan. Review of "Killer Queen." *Melody Maker*, October 26, 1974.

Jones, Lesley-Ann. "Bohemian Rhapsody Was Freddie Mercury's Coming Out Song." *The Wire*, April 9, 2017.

Kent, Nick. Review of *Queen*. *New Musical Express*, January 26, 1974.

Lee, Chris. "*Bohemian Rhapsody*'s Chaotic, Eight-Year Odyssey to the Screen." *Vulture*, November 1, 2018.

McCormick, Neil. "Brian May Interview: Freddie Is in My thoughts Every Day." *The Telegraph*, March 9, 2011.

Melley, Brian. "Freddie Mercury Auction Nets $15.4 Million." *Fortune*, September 6, 2023.

Moylan, Brian. "At Freddie Mercury's Estate Auction, the Rich Go Ga Ga." *Vulture*, September 8, 2023.

O'Malley, Sheila. Review of *Bohemian Rhapsody*. RogerEbert.com, November 2, 2018.

"The Oral History of the *Wayne's World* 'Bohemian Rhapsody' Scene." *Rolling Stone*, February 15, 2022.

Peisner, David. "'Robbie Ruined Our Song—He's No Freddie,' Says Queen Bassist." *Sun*, April 21, 2001.

Romano, Aja. "*Bohemian Rhapsody* Loves Freddie Mercury's Voice. It Fears His Queerness." *Vox*, January 6, 2019.

Runtagh, Jordan. "Freddie Mercury's Final Music Video: Director Rudi Dolezal Remembers." *People*, February 20, 2019.

Rush, Don. "Part 2: The Queen Tapes." *Circus*, March 17, 1977.

Stewart, Tony. Review of *A Night at the Opera*. *New Musical Express*, November 22, 1975.

Stewart, Tony. Review of *Sheer Heart Attack*. *New Musical Express*, October 26, 1974.

Sutcliffe, Phil. "Happy and Glorious? (Brian May Interview)." *Q*, March 1991.

Thomas, David. "Their Britannic Majesties Request." *Mojo*, August 1999.

Walker, Tim. "Queen Drummer Roger Taylor Says *We Will Rock You* Musical Is 'Crass.'" *The Telegraph*, October 11, 2013.

Webb, Julie. "The Contents of Freddie Mercury's Pants Are His Alone. They Belong to Him and to No-One Else." *New Musical Express*, November 4, 1974.

Webb, Julie. "Limp-Wrist Section: (Please Read with Camp Accent, Stressing Every Second Word." *New Musical Express*, September 27, 1975.

Webb, Julie. "Queen." *New Musical Express*, March 16, 1974.

Wiffen, Paul. "Queen: A Night at the Opera." *Sound on Sound*, June 2002.

BOOKS

Blake, Mark. *Is This the Real Life? The Untold Story of Queen*. Cambridge, MA: Da Capo Press, 2010.

Blake, Mark. *Freddie Mercury: A Kind of Magic*. Milwaukee, WI: Backbeat Books, 2016.

Blake, Mark. *Magnifico! The A to Z of Queen*. London: Nine Eight Books, 2021.

Hince, Peter. *Queen Unseen: My Life with the Greatest Rock Band of the 20th Century*. London: John Blake Publishing, Ltd., 2011.

Hutton, Jim, and Tim Wapshott. *Mercury and Me: An Intimate Memoir by the Man Freddie Loved*. London: Bloomsbury, 2019.

Jones, Lesley-Ann. *Mercury: An Intimate Biography of Freddie Mercury*. New York: Touchstone, 2011.

Lemieux, Patrick, and Adam Unger. *The Queen Chronology*, 2nd ed. Toronto: Across the Board Books, 2018.

Macdonald, David, and Thomas Williams, eds. *Freddie Mercury: A World of His Own*, London: Sotheby's, 2023.

May, Brian. *Queen in 3-D*. London: London Stereoscopic Company, 2018.

May, Brian, and Simon Bradley. *Brian May's Red Special: The Story of the Home-Made Guitar that Rocked Queen and the World*. London: Welbeck, 2020.

Purvis, George. *Queen: Complete Works*. London: Titan Books, 2018.

Reynolds, Simon. *Shock and Awe: Glam Rock and Its Legacy, from the Seventies to the Twenty-First Century*. New York: Dey St., 2016.

Richards, Matt, and Mark Langthorne. *Somebody to Love: The Life, Death and Legacy of Freddie Mercury*. San Francisco: Weldon Owen, 2016.

Rock, Mick. *Shot! By Rock: The Photography of Mick Rock*. New York: Weldon Owen, 2022.

Sheffield, Norman J. *Life on Two Legs: Setting the Record Straight on Queen, the Beatles, Elton and Bowie and the Ultimate Rock Studio, Trident*. London: Trident, 2013.

Smith, Jacky, and Jim Jenkins. *Queen: As It Began*. London: Omnibus Press, 2022.

Sutcliffe, Phil. *Queen: The Ultimate Illustrated History of the Crown Kings of Rock*. Minneapolis: Voyageur Press, 2011.

Warwick, Neil, Jon Kutner, and Tony Brown. *The Complete Book of the British Charts: Singles and Albums*. London: Omnibus Press, 2004.

Whitburn, Joel. *Joel Whitburn Presents Top Pop Singles Vol. 1: 1955–1989*. Menomonee Falls, Wisconsin: Record Research, 2021.

Whitburn, Joel. *Joel Whitburn's Top Pop Albums 1955–2016*. Menomonee Falls, Wisconsin: Record Research, 2018.

FILM

A Night at the Odeon (concert film)

Bohemian Rhapsody (feature film)

Classic Albums: The Making of A Night at the Opera (documentary)

The Freddie Mercury Tribute Concert (concert film)

Inside the Rhapsody: Queen (documentary)

Live at Wembley Stadium (concert film)

Making of The Prophet's Song (documentary)

The Magic Years (documentary)

The Making of a Masterpiece: Bohemian Rhapsody (documentary)

Queen Rock Montreal & Live Aid (concert film)

MISCELLANEOUS

Queen: The Inside Story (*Mojo Classic* magazine, 2005)

Queen (*Uncut The Ultimate Music Guide* magazine, 2023)

Queen radio interview, BBC Radio 1, December 24, 1977.

Screen Rant Plus, "Penelope Spheeris Interview: Wayne's World," YouTube, February 3, 2022.

WEBSITES

brianmay.com

deaky.net

queenchat.boards.net

queenconcerts.com

queenlive.ca

queenonline.com

queenpedia.com

queensongs.info

queenvault.com

rocksbackpages.com

setlist.fm

wikipedia.org

youtube.com

Image Credits

A = all, B = bottom, L = left, M = middle, R = right, T = top

Alamy Stock Photos: 13L (PA), 15 (Sean Dempsey), 16L (Archivio GBB), 25R (Mirrorpix), 31B (PA Images), 46T (Phil Rees), 58–59 (Pictorial Press), 62T (Pictorial Press), 66T (sjvinyl), 67 (tracksimages.com), 74–75 (Martyn Goddard), 83 (Pictorial Press), 87 (Pictorial Press), 91R (Collection Christophel), 92 (Goddard Archive), 100–101 (Goddard Archive), 111T (tracksimages.com), 114–115 (Goddard Archive), 116 (Goddard Archive), 117 (f8 archive), 118–119 (Goddard Archive), 125T (Impress), 125B (Paramount Pictures/RGR Collection), 127 (Featureflash Archive), 128 (dpa), 129 (Stephen Chung), 133 (Goddard Archive), 143 (Mirrorpix), 146 (ilpo musto), 147T (ilpo musto), 150 (makasana photo), 155A (Mirrorpix), 162 (GK Films/New Regency Pictures/Queen Films Ltd./Tribeca/Album).

Robert Alford: 2, 57R, 73, 77.

Associated Press: 126 (Kathy Willens), 154 (Neil Munns), 158 (Stefan Puchner/picture-alliance/dp), 159 (Efrem Lukatsky), 160 (Rob Griffith).

Creative Commons: 46B (Steve Guess/CC by 2.0), 47 (Ewan Monroe).

Getty Images: 4 (Michael Ochs Archives), 8 (Mark and Colleen Hayward/Redferns), 12 (Michael Putland/Hulton Archive), 14 (Ron Galella), 16R (Mark and Colleen Hayward/Redferns), 17 (Mark and Colleen Hayward/Redferns), 19 (Mirrorpix), 21 (Michael Putland/Hulton Archive), 23 (Michael Putland/Hulton Archive), 25L (Mark and Colleen Hayward/Redferns), 28–29 (Michael Putland/Hulton Archive), 35 (David Redfern/Redferns), 40 (Mark and Colleen Hayward/Redferns), 44 (Chris Walter/WireImage), 49 (Ian Dickson/Redferns), 50 (David Tan/Shinko Music/Hulton Archive), 51 (Jim Steinfeldt/Michael Ochs Archives), 52 (Ian Dickson/Redferns), 57L (*Guitarist Magazine*/Future), 63 (Gus Stewart/Redferns), 78 (TPLP), 81 (Andrew Putler/Redferns), 82 (Andrew Putler/Redferns), 85 (Ian Dickson/Redferns), 86L (M. McKeown/Hulton Archive), 94 (Erica Echenberg/Redferns), 97TL (TPLP), 99 (George Wilkes Archive/Hulton Archive), 103 (Keystone/Hulton Archive), 104–105 (Andrew Putler/Redferns), 110 (Michael Putland/Hulton Archive), 111B (Keystone/Hulton Archive), 113 (Koh Asebe/Shinko Music/Hulton Archive), 120 (PA Images), 123 (TPLP), 130 (RB/Redferns), 138T (Steve Jennings/WireImage), 149 (Dave Hogan/Hulton Archive), 157 (KMazur/WireImage).

IconicPix: 31T (Andre Csillag), 64 (Ian Dickson), 68 (Ian Dickson), 72 (Ian Dickson), 1239 (Marc Villalonga/Dalle).

Jim Kozlowski/Frank White Photo Agency: 41M.

Quarto Publishing Collection: 6, 7, 11T, 24T, 24B, 27A, 29T, 29M, 33B, 34T, 34M, 35B, 37TL, 37TR, 48, 56L, 56M, 62B, 66B, 67B, 70BR, 71, 75B, 76M, 76B, 80, 84, 86R, 89A, 91L, 93A, 97ML, 97R, 105T, 106TL, 108A, 109A, 112, 122A, 132BA, 134A, 136–137A, 138BA, 140–141A, 142, 145A, 147MR, 147BR, 148T, 148M, 152–153A, 160B, 161, 163, 164, 166A

©Brannon Tommey/www.photosets.net: 35TL, 35TR, 70BL, 106TR, 107A, 132ML, 135TL, 135TR.

Laurens Van Houten/Frank White Photo Agency: 37M, 38–39, 42–43.

Frank White/Frank White Photo Agency: 33R.

About the Author

GILLIAN G. GAAR has written for numerous publications around the world, including *Mojo*, *Rolling Stone*, and *Goldmine*. Her previous books include *She's a Rebel: The History of Women in Rock and Roll*, *Entertain Us: The Rise of Nirvana*, *Return of the King: Elvis Presley's Great Comeback*, and *World Domination: The Sub Pop Records Story*. Her other works for Motorbooks include *Elton John at 75* and *Bruce Springsteen at 75*. She lives in Seattle.

Index

A

Abbey, Peter, 11
Abbey Road Studios, 12
"Afternoon Delight," 126
All American Alien Boy (Hunter), 107
"All Right Now," 158, 161
"All the Young Dudes," 155
Allen, Kris, 159
American Idol, 159, 161
Andrews, Frank, 47
Angels, 70
"Another One Bites the Dust," 33, 134, 135, 152
Anthony, John, 11, 20, 22, 24
Apollo Theatre, 106
Appel, Mike, 22
Appleton, Mike, 98
Arden, Don, 43
Art, 32
Audience Award, 156
Austin, Mary, 20, 24, 52, 112, 129

B

"Back Chat," 135
Back to the Light (May), 152
Bad Company, 158
Bad News, 14
Baker, Roy Thomas, 7, 20, 22, 30, 34, 48, 50–51, 52, 54, 55, 60, 61, 107, 112, 134
Ballet for Life, A, 156
Band Aid, 142
Barcelona (Mercury), 24
Beach, Henry James "Jim," 43, 142, 144
Beach Boys, 26, 71
Beat Unlimited, 40

Beatles, 50, 69, 90
Béjart, Maurice, 156
Benton, Michael, 26, 30
"Best Selling 'A' Side," 122
Betancourt, Rómulo, 134
"Bicycle Race," 134
"Big Spender," 20, 37, 110
Biggles, 33
Black Sabbath, 14
Blake, Mark, 11, 61, 88, 135, 156
"Body Language," 135, 141
Bogie, Douglas, 20
"Bohemian Rhapsody," 6, 30, 48, 55, 60–61, 80, 88, 90, 96, 98, 102, 106–107, 122, 124, 126, 129, 142, 148, 152, 155, 156, 159, 160, 161, 165
Bohemian Rhapsody, 161–162, 164–165
Bonham, John, 40
Boomtown Rats, 142
Bowie, David, 34, 134, 154–155
Box of Flix, 98
Bradley, Simon, 56
Bray Studios, 153
Brenston, Jackie, 70
Brian May's Red Special (May and Bradley), 56
"Brighton Rock," 39, 75
"Bring Back That Leroy Brown," 39, 76
BRIT Award, 122, 126, 129, 147, 152, 153
British Phonographic Industry, 122
Brown, James, 40
Brown, Les, 11
Bubblingover Boys, 40
Budgie, 48

Bulsara, Freddie, 16. *See also* Mercury, Freddie
Bulsara, Jer, 156

C

Caballé, Montserrat, 24, 148
Cabaret, 155
Cable, Robin, 20, 26, 30
"Can't Get Enough," 158
Capital Radio, 96
Capitol Records, 141
Cars, 50
Carvey, Dana, 124, 134
"Cat-House," 70
Charisma, 20
Charles, Prince, 142
Charles, Ray, 40
Cheap Trick, 50
Chicago, 126
Classic Albums, 62
Classic Tracks, 53
Clockwork Orange, A, 111
Cohen, Mitchell, 109
Cohen, Sacha Baron, 162
Cook, Paul, 132
Cooper, Alice, 50
Coronation Street, 141
Cosmos Rocks, The, 158, 161
Cousin Jacks, 40
cover of album, 66
"Cowboy Song, The," 55
Crazy Eddie electronics stores, 135, 141
"Crazy Little Thing Called Love," 134, 141, 143, 154
Cream, 40
Cross, The, 14, 40

D

Dadd, Richard, 30
Daltrey, Roger, 40, 154
"D'Amor Sull'Ali Rosee" ("On Love's Rose Colored Wings"), 148
Daniel, Geoff, 40
Darkness, The, 50
Dax, Danielle, 70
Day at the Races, A, 50, 109, 111, 112
De Lane Lea Music Centre, 20
De Laurentiis, Dino, 134
de Smet, Wendy, 98, 110
Deacon, John, 6, 20, 26, 32–33, 39, 47–48, 54, 55, 60, 61, 66, 71, 73, 90, 96, 98, 134, 135, 142, 143, 144, 152, 153–154, 156, 158, 160, 164
"Death on Two Legs (Dedicated to . . .)," 54, 61, 66, 80, 102
Decca Records, 50
Def Leppard, 154, 155
Devo, 50
Diana, Princess, 142
Dietrich, Marlene, 90, 112
Dire Straits, 142
"Disco Demolition Night," 135
Disney Music Group, 148
"Do They Know It's Christmas?" 142, 143
Dobson, Anita, 14, 147
Doherty, Harry, 61, 96
"Doing All Right," 22, 55
Dolezal, Rudi, 148
Dominion Theatre, 156
Donegan, Lonnie, 12, 40
Donn, Jorge, 156
"Don't Stop Me Now," 134, 164
Douglas, Carl, 122

D'Oyly Carte Opera Company, 50
Drew, Paul, 107
"Driven by You," 148
Duncan, Robert, 20, 69

E
"Earth," 11
Edmunds, Dave, 48
Edney, Spike, 155, 156
Eisner, Michael, 148
Electric Lady Studios, 107
Electric Light Orchestra, 43
Elektra, 26, 48, 50, 107
Elizabeth II, Queen, 14
Elliott, Joe, 154
Ellis, Kerry, 14
Elstree Studios, 90
Elton, Ben, 156
EMI Records, 26, 34, 96, 98, 102, 122, 132
Everett, Kenny, 96, 102

F
Fairmont New Orleans hotel, 134
"Fairy Feller's Master Stroke, The," 30
"Fat Bottomed Girls," 12, 134
"Feel Like Makin' Love," 158
Firm, The, 158
Flamin' Groovies, 48
Flash Gordon, 134, 144
Fletcher, Dexter, 164
Foo Fighters, 156
For Your Entertainment (Lambert), 159
Formby, George, 86
Fowler, Ronnie, 34
Freddie Mercury: A World of His Own (auction), 129
Freddie Mercury Tribute Concert, 153–155
Free, 50, 158, 161

G
Game, The, 134–135, 141, 152
Garden Lodge, 148
Gasolin', 50
Geldof, Bob, 142
Genesis, 14
"Get Down Make Love," 132
Global Icon Award, 129
"God Save the Queen," 14, 48, 93, 96, 144
"Goin' Back," 26
"Good Company," 53, 86
"Good Old-Fashioned Lover Boy," 112
"Good Times Roll," 50
Gowers, Brian, 90
Grammy Hall of Fame, 126
Grammy Lifetime Achievement Award, 129
Grammys, 126, 129
Grant, Peter, 43
"Great King Rat," 22
"Great Pretender, The," 24
Greatest Hits, 122
Greatest Video Hits 1, 98
Grohl, Dave, 156
Grose, Mike, 19, 20
Grundy, Bill, 132
Guns N' Roses, 124, 154

H
Hamilton, "Diddy" David, 96
Hammer Film Productions, 153
"Hammer to Fall," 143
Hammersmith Odeon, 110
Harris, Johnathan, 70
Hawkins, Taylor, 40, 156
Hawkwind, 48
Hectics, 23
Hendrix, Jimi, 12, 16, 40, 107, 111, 112
"Heroes," 155
Hince, Peter, 110
Hollywood Records, 147–148
Hollywood's Walk of Fame, 129
"Honey Pie," 69
Hot Space, 134–135, 141, 161
Howell, Eddie, 24
Hunter, Ian, 107, 155
Hutton, Jim, 24, 88, 142, 144, 148, 164

I
"I Can Hear Music," 26
"I Got You (I Feel Good)," 40
"I Hear You Knocking," 48
"I Wanna Testify," 40
"I Want It All," 147, 154, 161
"I Want to Break Free," 33, 98, 141, 154
"I Was Born to Love You," 24
Ian and Belinda, 33
Ibex, 16, 18, 20, 24
"If You Leave Me Now," 126
Il Trovatore, 148
"I'm in Love with My Car," 54, 70, 161, 165
Immortals, 33
"In the Lap of the Gods," 39
"In the Midnight Hour," 40
Ingham, Jonh, 102, 106, 110
"Innuendo," 154
Innuendo, 40, 147–148
Inside the Rhapsody (documentary), 48, 55
"Is This the World We Created . . .?" 143
"It's a Beautiful Day," 152
It's Only Rock & Roll, 124
Ivor Novello award, 106, 122, 126

J
Jackson, Michael, 24, 134, 159, 161
Jazz, 50, 134, 144, 164
John, Elton, 33, 40, 43, 96, 155, 156
Johnny Quale and the Reactions, 40
Jones, Lesley-Ann, 88, 90, 96, 143
Jones, Steve, 132

K
Kansas, 40
"Keep Yourself Alive," 20, 26, 48, 98
Kent, Nick, 26
Kereluk, Cynthia, 158
Khalaf, Trip, 142
"Killer Queen," 37, 39, 102, 122
"Kind of Magic, A," 144
Kind of Magic, A, 144
Knebworth Park, 144
Knight's Tale, A, 160
Korniloff, Natasha, 98
"Kung Fu Fighting," 122

L
LA Forum, 134, 141
Lady Gaga, 14
Lambert, Adam, 6, 159, 161
Landmark video, 90–91
Langan, Gary, 53, 60–61
Langthorne, Mark, 52
Lansdowne Studios, 48
Laurence Olivier Awards, 156
"Lazing on a Sunday Afternoon," 52, 69, 76, 86, 109
"Leaving Home Ain't Easy," 14
Led Zeppelin, 43
Left Handed Marriage, The, 12
Lennox, Annie, 154
"Let Me Entertain You," 134
"Let Met in Your Heart Again," 161
"Liar, 98

Life on Two Legs (Sheffield), 43
Little Richard, 23
Live Aid, 141, 142–143, 164
Live at the Rainbow, 90
Live Killers, 134
Live Magic, 147
London Community Gospel Choir, 154
London Stereoscopic Company, 14
"Love Kills," 24, 161
"Love of My Life," 52–53, 84, 112, 165
Lyndyrd Skynyrd, 43

M

Made in Heaven, 80, 148, 152
Magic Johnson AIDS Foundation, 152
Magic Years (documentary), 55
Malek, Rami, 164
Man Friday & Jive Junior, 33
"Man from Manhattan, The," 24
Manor Studio, 109
Mansfield, Mike, 98
"March of the Black Queen, The," 30, 102
Martin, George, 50
Marx Brothers, 61, 109
May, Brian, 6, 7, 10–11, 12–14, 18–19, 20, 22, 24, 26, 30, 34, 39, 40, 47–48, 53–54, 55–56, 60, 61–62, 66, 69, 71, 73, 75–76, 80, 84, 86, 88, 93, 98, 102, 107, 109, 112, 124, 132, 134–135, 141, 142–143, 144, 147, 152, 154, 156, 158–159, 160, 161, 164
McCartney, Paul, 69, 143
Meat Loaf, 14
Mercury, Freddie, 16, 18–20, 22, 23–25, 26, 30, 32, 34, 37, 39, 43, 47–48, 52–55, 60–61, 66, 69, 71, 73, 75–76, 80, 84, 88, 96, 102, 106–107, 109, 110–111, 112, 122, 124, 126, 129, 132, 134–135, 141, 142–143, 144, 147–148, 152, 156, 161, 162, 164–165

Mercury and Me (Hutton), 144
Mercury Phoenix Trust, 155
Mercury Records, 11
Metallica, 154
Metropolis, 24, 98, 161
Michael, George, 154, 160
Michaels, Lorne, 124
"Millionaire Waltz, The," 112
Mineshaft, The, 164
Minnelli, Liza, 155
Minns, David, 52–53, 112
Miracle, The, 147
"Misfire," 33, 39, 71
Mitchell, Barry, 20
Mitchell, Mitch, 40
"Modern Times Rock 'n' Roll," 22, 40
"Mongolian Rhapsody," 55
Moon, Keith, 40
Morgan Studio, 50
Moroder, Giorgio, 24
Moseley, Diana, 144
"Mother Love," 148, 152
Mötley Crüe, 50
Motörhead, 48
Mott the Hoople, 30, 34, 107
Mountain Studios, 134, 148
Mr. Bad Guy (Mercury), 24, 161
MTV EMA Awards, 159, 161
MTV Europe Music Awards, 129
MTV Video Music Award, 122, 124
Murray, Neil, 153
Music Life, 47
Musicians Union, 141
"Mustang Sally," 70
"My Fairy King," 22
Myers, Mike, 124

N

Nash, Robin, 34
National Recording Registry, 129

Nazareth, 50
Neptune Productions, 20, 22
Never Mind the Bollocks (Sex Pistols), 132
New Opposition, The, 32
New Vaudeville Band, 69
News of the World, 26, 122, 132
Nichidai Kodo, 109
Night at the Odeon, A, 110–111
"Night Comes Down, The," 22
1984 (band), 11, 12, 16
Nippon Bodukan, 109
"No Turning Back," 33
"No-One But You (Only the Good Die Young)," 33, 156
Nordoff Robbins, 126
Novello, Ivor, 122
"Now I'm Here," 39, 75, 110, 154
Numan, Gary, 40

O

"Ogre Battle," 30, 102
Old Grey Whistle Test, The, 98, 110
Olympic Studios, 48
O'Malley, Sheila, 165
"One in a Million," 155
"One Vision," 144, 148
Opposition, The, 32
Osbourne, Ozzy, 50
Oscars, 164

P

Page, Jimmy, 158
Parliaments, 40
"Party at the Palace" concert, 14
"Pasadena," 86
Paterno, Peter, 148
Paul Rodgers Band, 158
"Penny Lane," 90
performances, legendary, 110–111
Pickett, Wilson, 40, 70

"Picking Up Sounds," 33
Plant, Robert, 154
"Play the Game," 135
Prenter, Paul, 144, 164
Presley, Elvis, 23, 40
"Procession," 30
Procol Harum, 122
promo films, 98–101
"Prophet's Song, The," 10, 53–54, 61, 80, 84, 102
"Psycho Legs," 54

Q

Quale, Johnny, 40, 41
Queen, 26, 144
Queen + Adam Lambert, 33
Queen + Adam Lambert "Rhapsody Tour," 6
Queen + Paul Rodgers, 33, 161
Queen Extravaganza, 161
Queen Forever, 161
Queen II, 30, 32, 34, 53, 55, 61, 90, 102
Queen Rocks, 156
Queen's Award, 122

R

"Radio Ga Ga," 40, 70, 98, 142, 144
Rainbow Theatre, 30, 38–39
Ray, 39
Reaction, The, 40, 41
Reactions, 40
Red Special, The, 56–57
Reid, John, 43, 52, 96, 112, 122, 144
Reynolds, Simon, 37
Rhodes, Zandra, 98, 134
Richards, Bill, 12
Richards, Matt, 52
Ridge Farm Studio, 47, 109
Roadrunners, 158
Rock, Mick, 90

Rock and Roll Hall of Fame, 126, 129, 156
"Rock Island Line," 12
"Rock with You," 159
"Rocket 88," 70
Rockfield Studios, 48, 55, 61
Rodgers, Paul, 6, 158–159, 161
Rolling Stones, 40
Romano, Aja, 165
Ronettes, 26
Rose, Axl, 155
"Rose Marie," 102
Roundhouse Studios, 10, 48, 96
Royal Albert Hall, 158

S

San Diego Sports Arena, 109
Santa Monica Civic Auditorium, 109
Sarm Studios, 48
SAS Band, 33
Saturday Night Live (*SNL*), 124, 141
Scorpio Sound, 48, 61
"Seaside Rendezvous," 53, 76, 86, 112
Sedlecká, Irena, 152, 156
"Seven Seas of Rhye," 34, 75
Sex Pistols, 132
Shanghai Express, 90
Shaw Theatre, 142
"Sheer Heart Attack," 132
Sheer Heart Attack, 32, 33, 34, 37, 39, 48, 61, 71, 76
Sheffield, Barry, 98
Sheffield, Norman, 43, 102
Sheffield, Norman and Barry, 20, 22
Shepperton Studios, 98
Shock and Awe (Reynolds), 37
"Show Must Go On, The," 147, 152, 156
Silver Clef Award, 126
Singer, Bryan, 164
Slash, 154
"Sleeping on the Sidewalk," 14

Small Faces, 43
Smashing Pumpkins, 50
Smile, 11, 14, 16, 19, 22, 40, 158
Smith, Chris, 11, 55
"Somebody to Love," 112, 154
Songwriters Hall of Fame, 129
Sound on Sound, 48, 60
Sounds of the Seventies, 26
Sour Milk Sea, 18, 24
South Africa, concerts in, 141, 143
Spector, Phil, 26
Spheeris, Penelope, 124
Spinal Tap, 154
"Spread Your Wings," 56
Springfield, Dusty, 26
Springsteen, Bruce, 22
Squier, Billy, 14
Staffell, Tim, 11, 12, 16, 22, 24
Stansfield, Lisa, 154
"Star Fleet," 14
Starland Vocal Band, 126
"Staying Power," 135
"Step on Me," 11
Stewart, Tony, 39, 106
Stone, Mike, 112
"Strawberry Fields Forever," 90
Sunbury Pop Festival, 30
Sutcliffe, Phil, 106
Swan Song Records, 43
"Sweet Lady," 54, 61, 75, 102, 106

T

T. Rex, 50
Talking of Love (Dobson), 14
Taylor, Elizabeth, 154
Taylor, Roger, 6, 11, 18, 22, 23, 26, 34, 40–41, 47–48, 53, 54, 60, 61, 66, 69–70, 73, 75–76, 88, 93, 96, 98, 102, 106, 107, 110, 111, 132, 142, 144, 147, 148, 152, 154, 156, 158–159, 160, 161, 164, 165

Temperance Seven, The, 86
"Tenement Funster," 39, 40
"Teo Torriatte (Let Us Cling Together)," 112
Terrence Higgins Trust, 148
Testi, Ken, 20
Tetzlaff, Veronica, 71
Théâtre de Chaillot, 156
"There Must Be More to Life Than This," 161
"These Are the Days of Our Lives," 40, 129, 148, 152
"'39," 54, 73, 111
Thomas, David, 14
"Tie Your Mother Down," 14, 112, 154, 156
Today, 132
"Too Much Love Will Kill You," 155
Top of the Pops, 34, 90, 102
tour dates, 166
T'Pau, 50
"Transit 3," 32
Trident, 11, 20, 22, 26, 30, 43, 48, 50, 102
"Turn on the TV," 40

U

U2, 154
UK Music Hall of Fame, 129, 158
"Under Pressure," 33, 134, 141, 154, 161
Ure, Midge, 142

V

Van Halen, Eddie, 14
Verdi, 148
Vicious, Sid, 132

W

Ward, Kingsley and Charles, 48
Wat Disney Company, 147–148
Wayne's World, 122, 124–125, 152
"We Are the Champions," 132, 143, 144, 155, 159, 161
"We Will Rock You," 14, 56, 129, 132, 143, 155, 156, 160, 161
We Will Rock You (musical), 156
Webb, Julie, 34, 37, 61
Welch, Chris, 43
Wembley Stadium, 144, 153, 161, 164
Wessex Studios, 132
Whishaw, Ben, 164
"White Queen (As It Began)," 30
Whitman, Slim, 102
Williams, Robbie, 160
"Winchester Cathedral," 69
"Winter's Tale, A," 152
Works, The, 141, 152, 161
Wreckage, 16, 24

Y

Yeadon, Terry, 20
"You Can't Take My Boyfriend's Woody," 70
"You Don't Fool Me," 152
"You Nearly Did Me In," 107
"You Take My Breath Away," 111, 112
Young, Paul, 152
"You're Driving Me Crazy," 86
"You're My Best Friend," 33, 54, 61, 71, 109, 111, 122

Quarto.com

© 2025 Quarto Publishing Group USA Inc.
Text © 2025 Gillian Gaar

First Published in 2025 by Motorbooks, an imprint of The Quarto Group, 100 Cummings Center, Suite 265-D, Beverly, MA 01915, USA.
T (978) 282-9590 F (978) 283-2742

All rights reserved. No part of this book may be reproduced in any form without written permission of the copyright owners. All images in this book have been reproduced with the knowledge and prior consent of the artists concerned, and no responsibility is accepted by producer, publisher, or printer for any infringement of copyright or otherwise, arising from the contents of this publication. Every effort has been made to ensure that credits accurately comply with information supplied. We apologize for any inaccuracies that may have occurred and will resolve inaccurate or missing information in a subsequent reprinting of the book.

This book has not been licensed or approved by Queen, by the band's management, or by any of the band's individual members. This is an unofficial publication.

Motorbooks titles are also available at discount for retail, wholesale, promotional, and bulk purchase. For details, contact the Special Sales Manager by email at specialsales@quarto.com or by mail at The Quarto Group, Attn: Special Sales Manager, 100 Cummings Center, Suite 265-D, Beverly, MA 01915, USA.

30 29 28 27 26   1 2 3 4 5

ISBN: 978-0-7603-8842-6

Digital edition published in 2025
eISBN: 978-0-7603-8843-3

Library of Congress Cataloging-in-Publication Data

Names: Gaar, Gillian G., 1959- author.
Title: Queen & A night at the opera : 50 years / Gillian G. Gaar.
Other titles: Queen and A night at the opera
Description: Beverly, MA : Motorbooks, 2025. | Includes bibliographical references and index. | Summary: "In Queen and A Night at the Opera, rock historian Gillian Gaar takes a deep dive into the iconic band's breakthrough album with a beautiful, slipcased gift book"—Provided by publisher.
Identifiers: LCCN 2024039646 | ISBN 9780760388426 | ISBN 9780760388433 (ebook)
Subjects: LCSH: Queen (Musical group). Night at the opera. | Rock music—England—1971-1980—History and criticism. | Progressive rock music—England—History and criticism.
Classification: LCC ML421.Q44 G23 2025 | DDC 782.42166092/2--dc23/eng/20240827
LC record available at https://lccn.loc.gov/2024039646

To Susan Despenich and Darcelle Zanzibar and that long-ago summer of 1981

Cover Image: Roger Taylor, Freddie Mercury, Brian May, and John Deacon pose for an Electra Records publicity still to promote their tour of Japan in 1975.
Front endpaper: Queen took a break from recording *A Day at the Races*, their follow up to *A Night at the Opera*, to make a few special appearances in the UK, including a show in Cardiff, Wales, on September 10, 1976.
Rear endpaper: Freddie in Cardiff, Wales, September 10, 1976. *A Night at the Opera*'s success had finally made him the star he'd always dreamed of becoming. He's still considered one of rock's finest lead singers, as well as a superlative showman.
Title Page: Queen's regal lead singer, Freddie Mercury, at the band's shows at London's Rainbow Theatre in 1974, the first Queen shows to be filmed.
Table of Contents: Queen in 1975, the year *A Night at the Opera* made them superstars.

Design: Cindy Samargia Laun
Book Cover Photo: Michael Ochs Archives/Getty Images

Printed in China